Etchings 36.1

Literary and Fine Arts Magazine of the
University of Indianapolis
Fall 2023

UNIVERSITY OF INDIANAPOLIS

1400 E. Hanna Ave.
Indianapolis, IN 46227

Cover Design by Etchings Staff
Cover Art by Alyssa Todd
Printed by IngramSpark
etchings.uindy.edu

Editorial Staff

Submissions Editor

Abigail Bailey

Managing Editor

E. Alexander Phillips-Hedge

Design Editor

Sierra Brooke Durbin

Senior Editor

Amber Phillips

Editors

Camille Dobbs
Emma Knaack
Emily Ratliff

Faculty Advisor

Liz Whiteacre

Table of Contents

***CW is short for Content Warning. Please read and review these pieces with caution.**

***... in a right bottom corner means a poem continues onto the next page.**

Colophon

Interior text is set in the Garamond font family.
The cover font is Rasa.

Letters from the Staff

"I am so glad to have been given the opportunity to step into the role of submissions editor again for this issue 36.1. I have enjoyed organizing and reading through all of the submissions, and I cannot help but be so proud of our campus community for its creativity! As you, the reader, are going through this magazine, please note that there are pieces with content warnings marked by a CW note. We want to make sure that our readers are comfortable, so please be advised that there are pieces in this issue that contain uncomfortable subjects."
- Abigail Bailey

"Walking in on the first day of this semester, I had no idea what to expect when working on the 36.1 *Etchings* staff. This experience has helped me understand the voting process of judging pieces of art. Personal taste plays a much greater role in this process than I had ever imagined. I now know as an author, my writing will not hit the goal for everyone and that is okay. Someone is cheering on your work. Stay creative and keep producing art."
- Amber Phillips

"A lot of work went into this process, and it is certainly exhilarating. There are many incredible pieces included, and I loved being able to go through them all and honor them. It's certainly nice being able to see the final product of a semester's work!"
- Camille Dobbs

"I felt like the development of this issue has been a challenge completely different from the previous three issues that I worked on before 36.1; however, I hope that this difficulty pays off and the final product shines through to the audience."
- E. Alexander Phillips-Hedge

"Every year I'm thankful to be on staff for *Etchings* and create a unique magazine with a range of submissions. What I want readers to know is that you could be someone in this magazine, you just have to put yourself out there. You may fail over and over, but that doesn't demise your talent or the possibility of you making it big one day. Take a chance and submit your work."
- Emma Knaack

"Being on the staff of *Etchings Magazine* has been valuable for me, as I have learned a lot about magazine production and what it is like to work as a member of a team. I look forward to applying this knowledge and experience in the future when necessary."
- Emily Ratliff

"Last semester, I had the opportunity to start building my skills in Adobe InDesign during the ENGL 479: Book Publishing course. I am proud of all the hard work and dedication I have put into my first semester on the editorial staff of *Etchings Magazine*, and I am honored to have my first leadership role as Design Editor. I struggle with social anxiety, so this was a big step for me to facilitate discussions during the production process and lead the team through all stages of the masterfile's development. Overall, I enjoyed the experience and being able to experiment with my artistic eye and attention to details. I care about each artist's work being shared with the campus community in the way they intended for their pieces to be seen so my perfectionism came in handy while creating issue 36.1."
- Sierra Brooke Durbin

Lullaby, Andante

Sarinitty Woodruff

Halfway to sleep, I found my headspace tenanted
by a dry wind and Black-eyed Susans

If you've never seen them before, from a distance,
you'd think they were wilting Sunflowers—

If I walked my body ways away from my mind
I might come to love myself, see me in a different light

Love the four thousand manic ideas settling inside
Hate the four thousand manic ideas seeping out

Weariness stamps the bottlebrush grass further
through the mush mud of muggy summers

There, in the small scene, I was a small mind running
through sprinklers and watching my grandma smile over her
    shades

Through the breeze, I watched my thick curls sprout in
    volume like
planted pumpkins in autumn, waiting for change in changing
    seasons

In Indiana, seasons are never rooted in one point of weather
And I can never stick my head onto one point of resolution

Drowsy memories are the stickiness of homemade, pre-
    baked
peanut butter fudge keeping my heart in place when my brain
    isn't

Just as I see an old relative shouldering me to pick off a
    cherry tree—
My eyelids finally drift down in pitch darkness to shut

And I let them.

Illustrations for Poetry Prize

These are solicited illustrations, selected by the *Etchings* staff, from work submitted by Art & Design Photography students.

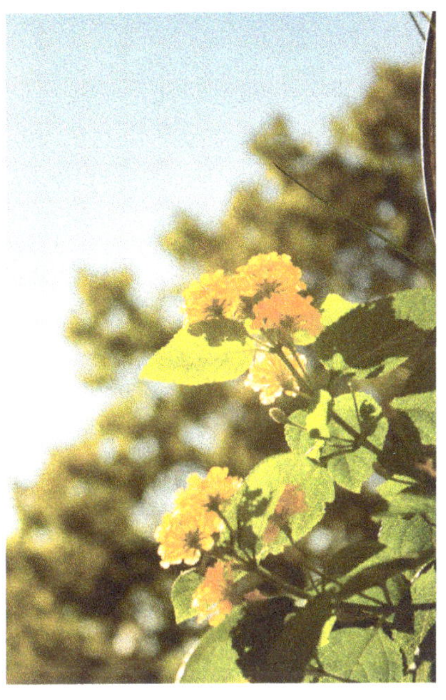

Blooming Warmth

Reid Bannec

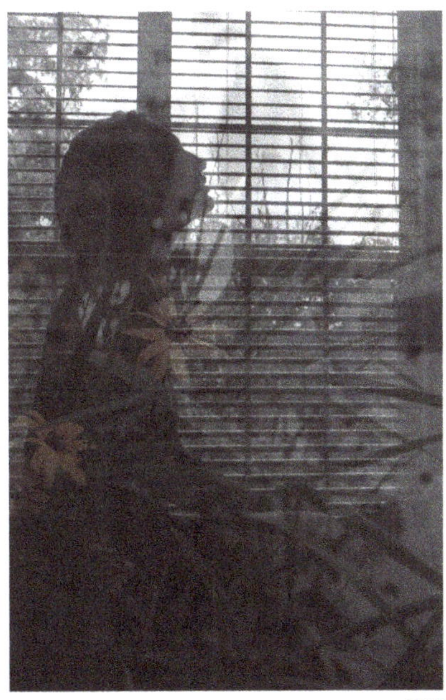

Dream

Elizabeth Dubak

2023 Roberta Lee Brooker Prize

The Sanctity of Dreams

Alrielle Viewegh

CW: Domestic Violence, Graphic Imagery

Regina Harte died today. She had been sick for weeks, coughing up blood and unsuccessfully trying to hide it in a dark red handkerchief. Just after lunch, she excused herself after coughing blood into her food. Then, she started to lose her balance. She didn't get back up once she hit the cement floor. Instead, her body tensed as though she were being electrocuted. Her face reddened; her eyes bulged out of her skull. She started crying blood. The rest of the women and I stood frozen in the factory, helpless to the scene that we had all seen too many times before. At least half of the women lost their mothers to this virus—to the Femm—already, and those who hadn't would likely lose them soon. Regina's back arched and her limbs stiffened in a robotic manner. We ceased to breathe and dropped our eyes to the floor. She died silently. Blood slowly trickled out from the holes all around her body. Blood mixed with the sterile smell of the factory. When a baby started crying, I jumped in surprise. Its cry was an alarm, forcing the other women back to work. A woman slowly walked to the bright red phone next to call the cleanup crew. As I cradled a baby at a station close to Regina's body, I watched another woman, no more than ten feet away from me, grab a baby blanket off of the shelf and drape it over Regina's face. My eyes followed the woman as she walked away.

The day shift ends at five, and I walk home with a warm sun slowly setting on my back. Fifteen feet ahead of me walks the woman who covered Regina. She's let her dark hair out of its bun, and it now dangles free in the middle of her back. Peeking out from the hem of her sleeve is a faint bruise, newly forming, and I have a faint feeling that she wears it as a badge. She's new to the factory, so I guess that's why she doesn't know the bodies are never covered. It just seems pointless. Some of the women took bets once on how many women would die in a week at the factory. No one won. I have to keep myself from shivering at the thought as I trail behind the woman. She walks calmly, barely noticing the throngs of people scurrying up and down the dull gray sidewalk.

As we are walking, the woman and I instinctively cross to the other side of the street as we pass two women who look like they're sleeping on the sidewalk, but the pools of blood around them give them away. Our feet carry our legs forward, moving us to the sidewalk where we have to push through throngs of men and women waiting for a room to become available for the ritualistic insemination facility. I'll have to visit this facility at least fourteen times with the seven *strangers* I've been matched with for procreation. I've crossed the street once or twice to avoid bodies, and I'm only a few feet behind the woman as she enters and disappears into the crowd. I dive in after her. Bodies push and press against me from every angle. My feet are stepped on, I trip once or twice, and I'm even elbowed once in the ribs. Yet none of this makes me yelp and falter with fear like I do when a sneaking hand reaches up and grabs my chest. The crowd bustles around me, hiding the hand and its perpetrator. No one bothers to look my direction, so I fold my arms around myself and force my body through the rest of the crowd. I don't make it out without being touched two more times. When I emerge, I see the woman further ahead of me, walking without hesitation.

Baby blanket woman lives three doors down from Eric's apartment. I never knew that or, at least, I never noticed *her*. My eyes flick up from the carpet I've been staring at just in time to see the woman slip into her door. A smile jumps onto my face as Eric's hand circles below my hip, pulling me around to face him. He meets my smile, eyes creasing at the corner, as he unlocks his apartment door. I step in first as the door swings open, leaving my keys in the green ceramic bowl Eric set out for me when we were matched and married a few months ago. My hands are already moving mechanically to make dinner as he steps in, takes off his coat, and sets his briefcase by the black table holding up my green ceramic bowl. He shifts my keys in the bowl, straightening them, before he closes the door behind him. His footsteps echo as he approaches me. I stiffen just before his hand reaches my lower back. My muscles are full of lactic acid as I turn my head to him. He pecks me on the mouth, his hand lingering on my back before he steps away again. When he does, it brushes my butt.

My back aches and nausea wrecks my stomach, but I rush to make dinner. Eric emerges from the bathroom just as I dish up the food. He sits down in the chair closest to the door, so I am forced to sit here facing him and the door, trying to decide how I am possibly going to get through dinner without fighting for escape. My limbs fidget in silent protest.

"Is something wrong?"

I hesitate before I speak.

"A woman covered the body today with a cloth."

"So?"

"No one ever does that."

"Dead is dead no matter if they're covered or not."

"But *this* felt different."

"Women die every day, Verity, let it go."

I swallow a lump that has formed in my throat. My mouth and tongue feel like I've licked sand. It makes my nausea worse.

After dinner, Eric hands me two prenatal vitamins and a glass of water. He watches me swallow them with his boring eyes before he herds me into the bedroom. There, my fingers begin to lose their dexterity as they try to unbutton the clasps on my clothes. Sometimes he has to do this for me because I am unable to make my joints work. I fall back onto the bed, letting agony wash over me.

I have to lay flat on the bed for twenty-five minutes before I can go to the bathroom. Eric doesn't let me shut the bathroom door; he hands me a pregnancy test and watches me pee on the plastic stick. I close my eyes as I pee to pray that pregnancy will never grace my body even though all of the fertility tests indicated that I am extremely fertile. That's why I've been matched with those seven other men. I have to have two children with each of those strangers for "repopulation purposes." These are the children sent to the factories, the children I take care of. They'll never know me, and I'll never know them. I can't tell if that's better or not. All of this is, of course, in addition to the children Eric will force me to carry and birth. *At least four*, as he's so lovingly reminded me. After the last of the urine trickles out of me, I gently shake the pee off the stick. Eric is already holding his hand out.

"Let me see it."

I hand it over, glancing at the negative test as I do.

That night, I dream of pink lines searing through the pregnancy test, cutting into my wrists like knives. I dream of a baby crying, and a young girl bleeding. I dream of hands bruising skin. I'm forced awake by the wave of nausea that rocks me. I stumble towards the bathroom, bracing my hands and arms along the walls to keep my body upright. I hear Eric flick on a light as I heave dinner into the toilet. Tears mix with the acidic sauce spilling out of me. My body shakes, forcing me to seize on the floor after my dinner is all gone. Fear and regret and guilt begin to solidify in my bones, but it is anger that finally forces me to my feet. My lips know four smiles, no more and no less. One for genuine happiness, one for fake happiness, one to feign ignorance, and one for lying. Each of these flashes before me in the mirror before I wipe my mouth. The smiles fade. I graze the hem of my shorts, revealing the bruises hidden behind their fabric. My stomach boils with heat. When I return to bed, anger forces me to not meet Eric's eyes. He switches off the lights, and his arm encircles my stomach.

My mother died silently and alone. I was probably the only one who noticed she was gone. The cleanup crew probably didn't even register that they were picking up another body, mopping up its blood. I never knew my father; she made sure of that. I was alone after she died. I've known the Femm longer than I knew her. I've known its threats and deaths. I've known I would be married off since half the age of puberty, a cow abused, forced to birth, and left to the mercy of the wolves. Just like me. I wish I knew how to protect myself. I wish she had taught me.

She left the factory early today. Now, I'm trying not to stare as I approach her on the street. She's facing me, but she hasn't looked at me. Something in my bones tells me she won't, and something in my muscles tries to compel me to walk on the other side of the street, the side away from the insemination facility, away from what has haunted, but I don't let my feet carry me away. Instead, I keep my gaze steady on her, steady on the horizon. She doesn't flinch as I come within a few feet of her; she doesn't even sway when the man she's with grabs her in a place I pray to never be grabbed.

"You belong to me," he growls.

He rips away from her. I jump to the side to avoid him. I can't see her expression as I keep walking home, but I can feel her eyes. Until this morning, the art of knowing you're being watched was a subconscious hum. Now I feel it like a freight train.

I'm beginning to feel less alone as we walk down the hallway to our apartments together. She is just a few feet behind me, and I feel her shoulder brush against my hair when she passes me. I watch her out of the corner of my eye, pretending to look for something in my purse, as she unlocks her door. My body freezes again as she turns on me.

"You saw what happened back there?" She asks.

"Yes."

"Good. Most people don't even notice."

"Why didn't you do anything?"

She laughs and closes the gap between us in five swift steps.

"Do you do anything when you're grabbed? Did you do anything when I was grabbed?"

My mouth suddenly feels so dry. Heat rises to my face, and I am forced to look down in shame. Only a second passes before the woman's hand raises my chin, my eyes meeting hers once more, and her hand rests on my shoulder.

"They can grab me, yell at me, use me, and no one will do a thing about it. The only person who is going to protect me is me, but I'll make them all regret it one day."

"How?"

I feel like a child. My eyes are lost in hers.

Her eyes are on me again. To keep myself from looking at her, my fingers fidget with the vial she gave me yesterday. I bump the bruises on my leg as my fingers twist around in my pocket, forcing me to hide a wince. Baby blanket woman clears her throat, prompting me to turn toward her. With a simple nod of her head, I am directed to the men in nurse's uniforms walking up and down the rows of babies. Their presence is scheduled, expected even, and I turn back to her in confusion. She nods again, so I am forced to not merely glance this time but study them. They stalk up and down the rows of babies like wolves. One man listens as another reads information off a clipboard. When he points at a baby, a third man writes it down. Once they have finished with a row, two more men break off from the group to wheel the babies out of the room. I don't realize how long I had been watching them until she brushes up against me.

"What are they doing?"

"What do you think?" she counters.

I pause. When she realizes I still don't understand, she

picks up the bottle of baby powder from my station and spews it onto the cold metal counter. With her pointer finger, she writes "DONATED" in the white powder. Our eyes meet as realization passes through me.

Baby blanket woman had awoken something in me. The cardboard box of my mother's old belongings is hidden amongst my socks in my bottom dresser drawer. I fold back the lid to see the first of three pictures of my mother and her friends staring up at me. I set them aside to pull out the slips of yellowing-white paper. Six gleam up at me. I grab one and read it. My mother's information dances across the page. The hospital tag sends shivers down my spine as I flip it over. "5.2 lbs., female" was written hurriedly on the back. In much neater letters, "donated" is written below my long-lost sibling's information. *Donated.* A pit settles into my stomach, one that I know will never dissipate.

We walk home together. We're about two feet apart, side-by-side, not talking, but we walk home together. Baby blanket woman and I walk straight through the hoard of men silently groping women as they wait to get into the insemination facility. She only brushes my hand once when I try to wrench away as a man reaches for me. I don't know if it's her way of comforting me, or if she's telling me to take it; we'll have our time. I'm still thinking of her hand brushing mine when we walk down the hallway of the apartment building, and my world starts to darken once more. Eric is waiting there, standing in front of his door, looking like he's in a particularly ugly mood. His hand immediately goes for my stomach, cupping what is his. She passes us as though I'm not even there. If I had been in her way, I am convinced she would have passed through me. Eric's hand feels unnaturally hot on me. I wriggle in discomfort, trying to get away from him, but it only makes his grip turn hard, almost painful, as he unlocks his apartment. He doesn't say a word as I start dinner, and the silence stretches until we are both eating. I'm facing the door.

"You've been acting strange the past few weeks," he says.

"I'm just tired."

"Maybe you should just quit your job."

I took a drink of water to save myself from responding.

"I think we should find you a new doctor, too. You look like shit."

"I'm just tired," I repeat again.

"How many men are you matched to again? Seven? You're required to have two kids with each, and I want four —*at least*—four boys. There's no way you can be a mother and keep working at that factory taking care of God knows whose kids."

I muster up my fourth smile almost as easily as I can lie. Eric pauses before he smiles back, but, when he does, he launches into what he's been doing at work, never bothering to actually check if I'm paying attention.

"And we got a new batch of test subjects in today. All Donated. The other doctors and I have a great amount of hope placed in them because, as I told you yesterday, we are implementing *my* plan for a cure with this batch. The older researchers keep talking about how my plan—"

"Donated?"

"Yeah, I've told you this."

"What does that mean?"

I switch to my third smile.

"We need subjects who might die from the Femm, so candidates who aren't even healthy enough to have a chance are donated. We need to figure out a plan to increase genetic diversity, to really fight this virus."

I swallow, expecting a lump to be lodged in my throat, but saliva slides down easily.

"It's all in the name of genetic diversity."

A dream of a young girl fills my mind as soon as my eyes close for the night. She's me, but she's also *her*, the one who's inside of me. She is running through a field of flowers, one I've never seen before, laughing and smiling. Her innocence is almost enough to draw me in and make me forget, but the dream turns violent. She falls, leaves cutting into her. I try to scream out, catch her, but my arms don't even reach halfway. Wolves are on the girl in seconds, tearing off her flesh in strips of bloody ribbons. The ribbons are strewn around her body as she writhes in pain. Only after she is stripped clean do they devour the rest of her. Then, they turn on me. I wake up sweating, shaking, and nauseous. Eric sleeps soundly next to me. If I blur my vision, he almost looks dead.

Baby blanket woman and I stand in the hallway of our apartment. She's unlocking her door as I wait for Eric.

"What's in the vial?" My voice breaks the silence.

"A special type of poison, my own concoction. A few drops will make you very ill, a lot of it will kill you. The residue is just as potent as the liquid. Every morning I put a few drops of it in the crotch of my pants, on the *outside* of my pants, so anyone who touches me there pays within a few days."

"So when you're touched…"

Her eyes meet mine, making my stomach leap and burn all at once. My fingers brush the vial in my pocket once to comfort myself.

"Are you infertile?" I ask. "I don't mean to be rude. It's just…we *have* to have kids."

"I've seen your bruises," she says. "I used to have bruises, too, but I couldn't survive that life. I've seen the scars on your wrists. I have scars."

"Where?"

She looks down, almost like she is directing me. My hand reaches into my pocket. Heat and discomfort are suddenly rising in me, and they are exacerbated when a hand presses into my stomach. I jump and whip around.

Eric turns me to the door, unlocking it.

"We only have to have two kids," I say.

Eric halts with the fork halfway to his mouth.

"You've been hanging out with that *woman* too much. Did you know I heard she left her husband after she had his kids? If he finds her, she deserves whatever is coming her way."

"Maybe he deserved to be left."

I never see his hand; I just feel my face burning. I cup my cheek with my own hands and stare at him from across the table. He won't meet my eyes. My vision is starting to blur, but I blink a few times, refusing to give him any sadistic satisfaction. Stupidly, I don't see what else I could lose.

I feel like I don't really need to tell this part of the story. We all know what's going to happen, and it feels like it's going to hurt again by talking about it. Some part of me thinks that talking about it will make a difference, but most of me knows that few people who actually hear me will listen. She would. I know she's going to die. She might even do it herself. My eyes will be there when she does.

Dinner with Eric was ritualistic, but things had still changed since he hit me. Now, he walked in the door before me, took my keys, and placed them in that green ceramic bowl, always making sure they were perfectly straight before he ushered me in, locking the door behind me. There was still the same robotic kiss, but the silence that pervaded his apartment was deafening. My ears rang every night. The sound drove me crazy, almost crazier than I had been feeling. Her face wouldn't leave my mind. She was all I could ever really see. I saw her in myself when I looked in the mirror. I saw her in the steam of whatever I was cooking. I saw her in the factory every day. Every day when I caught her looking at my new bruises and cuts, I felt something grow harder in me.

I see her now in the water running out of the kitchen sink. Eric's hand on my stomach calls me back to reality. I feel my stomach turn violently, but I smile up at him, the second smile stretching unnaturally. As we sit down for dinner, I try to convince myself that everything is fine, but I know the lie almost better than I know myself. Eric's fork drops on his plate with a clank, calling me back the final time. I meet his eyes. They're ugly and dark. Mad, even, but I fail to find fear in myself.

"Are you enjoying dinner? Lamb is actually one of my favorite foods."

"Oh, I didn't know."

"Have you ever slaughtered a lamb?"

"No."

"Well, they always cry."

My hand reaches for my pocket.

Dinner passes faster than I wanted it to. Nausea spreads throughout my body, forcing me to take another drink of water to keep anything from coming up. Eric sighs and stretches his arms out on either side of him, his lanky skin stretching to show the intersecting roadmap of green and blue veins stretching out from the hem of his white, short-sleeve undershirt. "Dinner was great."

Thanks for making it.

"Yeah."

I stand up. My chair pushes back from me, creating a jarring sound that juxtaposes violently against the silence that hangs about this apartment like the stench from meat left to rot too long in the trash can. His eyes are on me as I clear the table. Mechanical movements guide my limbs through the too familiar process. The dishes wash themselves in the sink. Leftover food is placed in containers for Eric's lunch. His eyes are on me the entire time. They feel different than hers. They are not safe and warm like hers. They are a violation cutting through the most vulnerable parts of me.

His chair scrapes against the floor as he slowly walks

over to the black table holding my green bowl or, at least, what used to be *mine*. Next to the bowl, he unscrews the lids off of the prenatal vitamins. Then, Eric pulls open the drawer under the green ceramic bowl, grabbing a pregnancy test. All of this is done painstakingly slow as I wait, a glass of water already in hand. He first gives me the pills, which I swallow with a gulp of water. I smile, open-mouthed, showing him the pills have been swallowed. Then, I am led into the bedroom. For the first time, my fingers manage to slip off all of my clothes. I look down my body, seeing a sea of colorful bruises, old and forming scars. I count every single second as I lie on the bed. When I am finished, I've made it to an hour's worth of seconds.

I get up, stumble, and fall into my pile of clothes on the floor. My fingers grasp the vial that's no larger than my pinky. I tuck it between my fingers and take the pregnancy test that Eric is holding out. His hand feels predatory as he places it on my stomach, guiding me into the bathroom. Eric smiles, his frame blocking the doorway, as he watches me pee. I hold eye contact with him even as my fingers slyly move, pouring the contents of the vial onto the plastic stick. The vial drops into the bowl of the toilet without a sound when I am done. Instead of shaking off the stick or wiping myself, I stand, holding out the stick to Eric. I don't need to see the results or look at Eric's face to know, I simply brush past him and climb into bed.

Urine is drying on my legs when Eric climbs into bed next to me. His hand is dry when it cups my stomach. It takes less than thirty seconds of me lying still on the bed, first smile and tears donning my face, to know fates are sealed. I can see her eyes on me—both of their eyes on me—as Eric takes his final breaths.

Illustrations for Fiction Prize

These are solicited illustrations, selected by the *Etchings* staff, from work submitted by Art & Design Photography students.

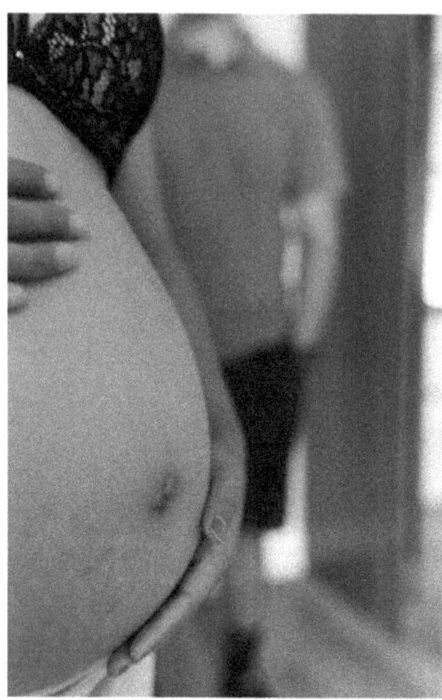

Can't Say NO

Hniang Te

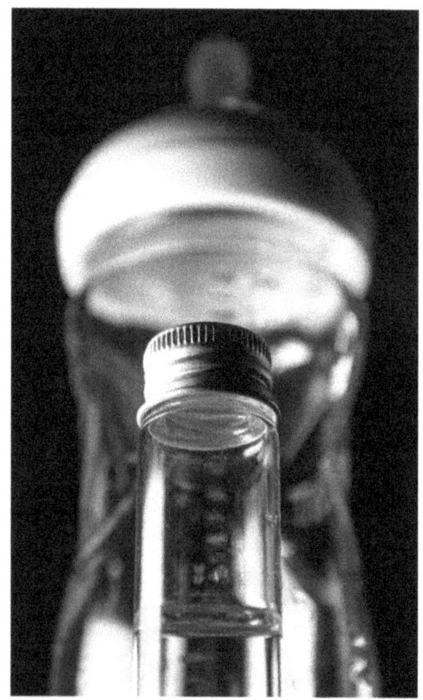

Looming

Lilli Keiper

2023 Winner in Studio Art

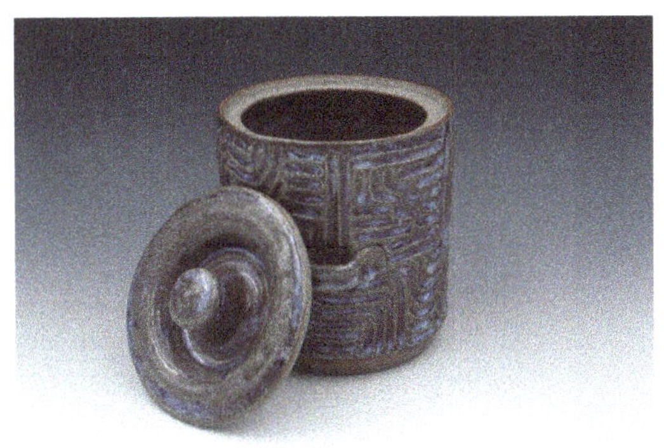

Carved Jar

Kaelyn Stettler

2023 Winner in Visual Communication

Woyzeck

Raegan Brinson

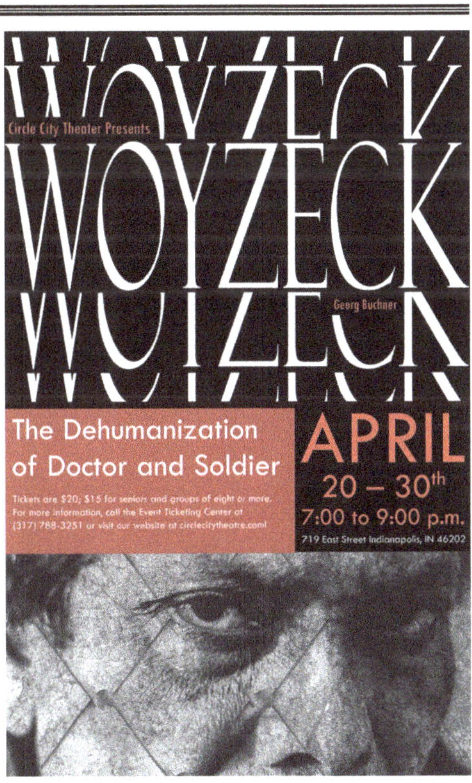

2023 Art Awards

The recipient of the **UIndy Anna Elizabeth Gott Memorial Art Award** was **Alyssa Todd**. This award, honoring outstanding senior art and design majors, was endowed as a memorial in 1978 by Anna's sister, Mary E. Gott. Anna Elizabeth Gott had traveled widely in her career with the federal government and, in doing so, developed a deep interest in the great masterpieces of world art. The UIndy Art & Design Faculty determine the recipient of this award.

The recipient of the **UIndy Mary E. Gott Award for Excellence in Art** was **Kensington Skaggs**. This award, honoring outstanding junior art and design majors, was endowed in 1984 by UIndy Professor Emeritus Robert Brooker and his wife, Ruth, as a tribute to Mrs. Brooker's aunt, Mary E. Gott. Mary, like her sister Anna, held a government post in Washington, D.C. and loved art. The UIndy Art & Design Faculty determine the recipient of this award.

Dorlis Gott Armentrout Award

Winner: "The Bridge" by Julia Johnson
From the first line, I knew this was a special story. In six words, Julia gives conflict, voice, and setting. "The Bridge"'s pace has a subtle suspense, leading the reader on graph by graph; this is not a story to put down until you get to the end. And who doesn't love a sympathetic speaker? Don't we all know an Opal?

Runner-Up: "The Birth of Lilith" by Olivia Cameron
This opens with some very effective parallelism, and I love that the piece is a conversation between two people: Lilith and her interviewer. I also appreciate that each read presents a different idea regarding who that interviewer might be. A curious bystander? A mother? The author?

Dorlis Gott Armentrout Award Judge

Jaclyn Youhana Garver is an author, poet, and journalist. Her first novel is scheduled to be published in fall 2024 by Lake Union Publishing, and she is represented by Savannah Brooks of KT Literary agency. Her story "The Butterfly Catcher" appeared in From Beyond Press's *The World Belongs To Us: An Anthology of Horror Stories About Bugs* in 2023. Her first poetry collection, the chapbook *The Men I Never*, was published in 2023 from Chicago's dancing girl press. Garver's current and previous freelance clients include *Cincinnati Magazine*, *Lifehacker.com*, *Harper College*, *Orange Coast College*, *Visit Fort Wayne*, and *Graphics Output*. Her Instagram handle is @jyogarver.

Interview with the Judge

EP: How do you conquer writer's block?

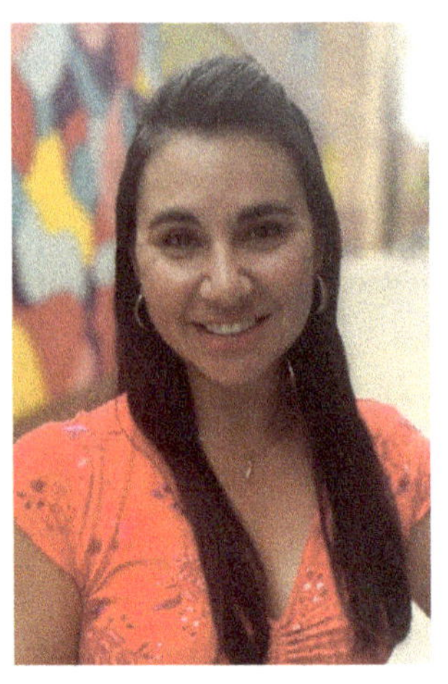

JYG: Oh, I love that image of conquering it—I wish writer's block made me feel like someone swinging a battle axe. For me, writer's block manifests as struggling to get my butt to the page. I feel lucky that it doesn't happen often, but when it does…oof. It happens when I'm feeling overwhelmed, whether that's because I am swamped at my day job or undergoing a personal upheaval. I deal with it by being kind to myself. I know that long-form first drafts are simply not going to happen during that time, but writing and editing poetry? Definitely. I'll also turn to writing-adjacent activities: reading, going to shows or museums, or listening to music. Absorbing others' art is deeply inspiring, and even if it doesn't spark creativity in the moment, there's nothing wrong with stockpiling inspiration.

EP: How do you find your voice as a journalist?

JYG: Years and years of writing! I studied newspaper journalism in college, and I remember professors being like, "Focus on the how-to, and the voice will come." I was deeply stubborn and thought, "Screw that, I'm going to have a voice now!" Yeah, it took years to realize it doesn't work like that. Voice is developed after writing tons and reading tons. You see what you like, what feels and sounds like *you*. The more I've gotten into creative work, especially poetry and novels, the more I've seen my voice continue to evolve in journalism, too. I'm braver than I used to be at taking risks and better understand what risks work to advance a story and which are simply flexing creative muscles for the sake of the flex.

EP: How does the writing you do in journalism inform your creative work?

JYG: I love interviewing people. The joy I get from being nosy means I love my creative research to come in the form of interviews, too. Here's an example from my first drawer novel (which will probably never see the light of day, but I cannot overstate the lessons I learned from it): One of the characters made wine at home. I don't know how to do that, but a friend does. So we met up. We chatted for hours, I took notes, and he gave me a thumb drive that outlined the process, too. I could have gotten that info from Google, but it couldn't compare to having a friendly expert in front of me spelling out how it all works, how much space the setup requires, what can go wrong, and how long it takes.

EP: How do you decide if an idea should turn into a poem or story?

JYG: Oh, this is an interesting question. I'm not sure I've ever sat with it as a decision! I suppose it depends on the goal of the piece. Do I want to honor a feeling or meaningful event? Poetry. Do I have a big-picture theme I want to explore because I'm not quite sure what I think about it? Novel. For example, I just got back from a work trip to Colorado and spent a good amount of time laughing that, holy cow, it's hard to breathe in that altitude. So I wrote a poem about breath. I didn't need more than a few stanzas to make it work. But my current novel-in-progress is about a topic I've pondered for over a decade—friendship break-ups, which is taking thousands of words to study.

EP: When do you know a poem or story you are working on is ready to submit to a publisher?

JYG: My general goal is, I want to get a piece to the point where I personally am unable to improve on it anymore. I like letting first drafts marinate for a bit so I can forget about it and reread with fresh eyes. I am incredibly lucky to have a number of generous friends who are spectacular writers and readers, and I love to get their input. I know I'm close to submitting when I'm starting to read the thing aloud. How does it sound? Is the rhythm musical? Do I accidentally use a certain word a bunch (one of mine is "just")? Are my metaphors surprising? Some of these questions, I can answer easiest after I hear the sentences aloud.

EP: What advice do you give to an emerging writer who's just starting to publish?

JYG: 1) Do your research. Every contest/agent/publisher wants something different. I've always told myself when I don't get accepted to something, I want it to be because the writing didn't resonate and not because I couldn't follow directions. 2) Don't take any of it personally! Which, admittedly, is tough—I mean, is there anything more personal than writing? Similarly, though, is there anything more personal than taste? You gotta let rejection slide off your back. A good way to do that is to submit to all the places. When you've got your story out with a dozen contests, it doesn't hurt so badly when you get a "no thanks" because you've got 11 more possibilities out there. Another POV that can help: Do you really want to work with a person/group who isn't giddy about what you do? Your publisher should be gaga over you.

Artemis

Breanna Emmett

You want this life
Children to behold you, adore you
You want a lover to take you apart
and fill you with every dream you've held
in that pretty little head of yours.
You want a life like every other woman.

I hold no love for my womb.

Even lacking life, an empty vessel,
it breathes fear into my heart,
a promise
that someday it will obliterate
the vow I've made to my dear moon goddess,
a vow to hold onto every jagged edge of myself,
to not wax or wane on this path.

You spit in the faces of the gods
by rejecting the power granted to your womb.
Your mind is so frivolous and fragile,
so young and impressionable.
You cannot know what you want.

Voices in the night whisper to me,
silenced by moonlit wind,
but still piercing,
a persistent prickling as prevalent
as a knife scraping between ribs.

...

You lack everything
but your stubborn pride.
What do you think you will gain
by rejecting tradition? You cannot fill
a heart with a broken legacy.

Your poor mother.
Have you not taken enough from her,
you wretched ingrate?

On quiet nights, when the wind is hollow
and the moon is nothing but a sliver of light,

I am Artemis.

A beast at home in forests of night,
wrapped in delicious solitude
a predator riddled with craters of scars,
relentless in her hunt
for a life of her choosing.

The Birth of Lilith

Olivia Cameron

CW: Sex, Violence
Dorlis Gott Armentrout Runner-Up

Where did you come from?
snakes and apples and freedom and knowing
and nakedness and fucking and touching
and choosing and running and screaming
and wildness and birthing and bleeding.

They call me Adam's first wife. (he only had one)

Want to hear a secret? (everyone does)

I gutted that bitch Eve.
I clawed through her, bottom to top
nails and teeth ripping into flesh
pushed myself into her torso
caging myself in her ribs.
(but I can't be caged)
This body wasn't big enough for the both of us.

Succubus

Olivia Cameron

CW: Sex

It is said that a succubus needs semen
to survive but I don't think sucking a boy off
on the school bus is any girl's reason to be alive.

As the wheels on the bus go
round and round, the guys are trashing
the girls that they begged to go down.

The girls wait at the bus stop, with bruises
on their knees, knowing that if you don't ride
the bus all the way "you're just a tease."

They are considered demons
in their own right. Daughters of Lilith,
born to cause mayhem and schoolyard fights.

So if it's monsters people want, monsters
they will be. For when someone's manhood
is in your mouth, knowing who has the power is easy.

Pandora's Box-HOPE

Alexis Darland

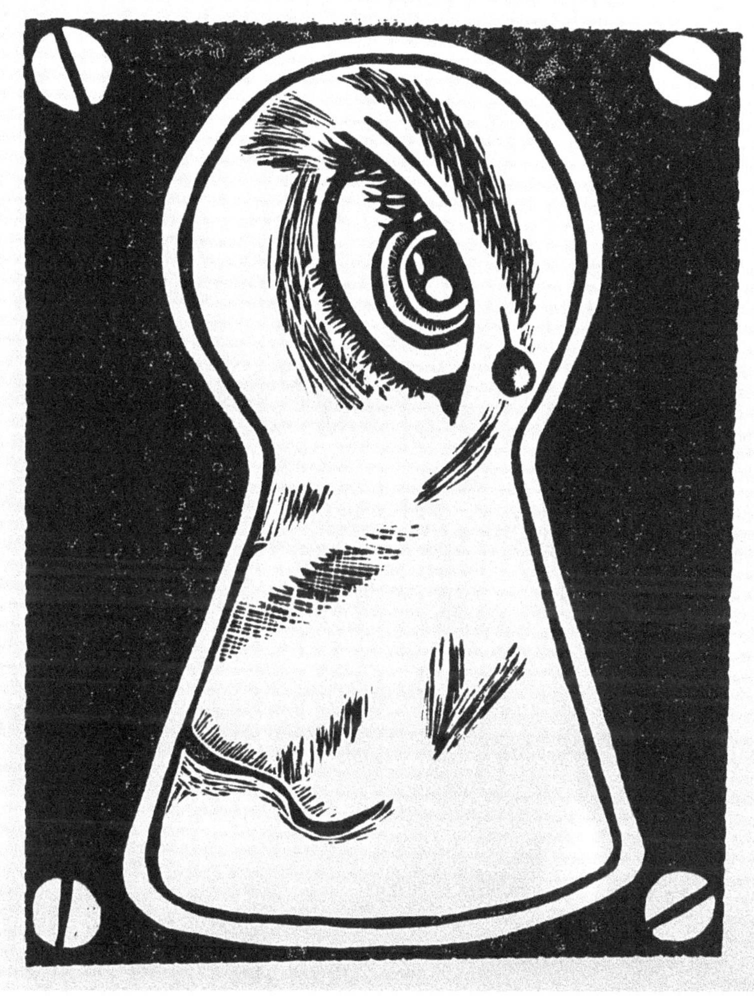

Venomous Lover

Danni Conn

Drawn to you,
not knowing
your love was venomous.

The thrill
        of not knowing.
Enticing
        at first.

Kiss or kill,
2 letters too close.

Your saliva spinning with
wicked venom.

Traveling through my body
entering the bloodstream,
        blood clotting,
        arrhythmic heartbeats.

Kept as prey
        once again.

You got me wrapped up
in your web of lies.
Escape seeming unattainable.

I cannot be captivated
by your venomous nature
anymore.

Can't you see
        you're killing me
s l o w l y

The Other Mother

Alyssa Todd

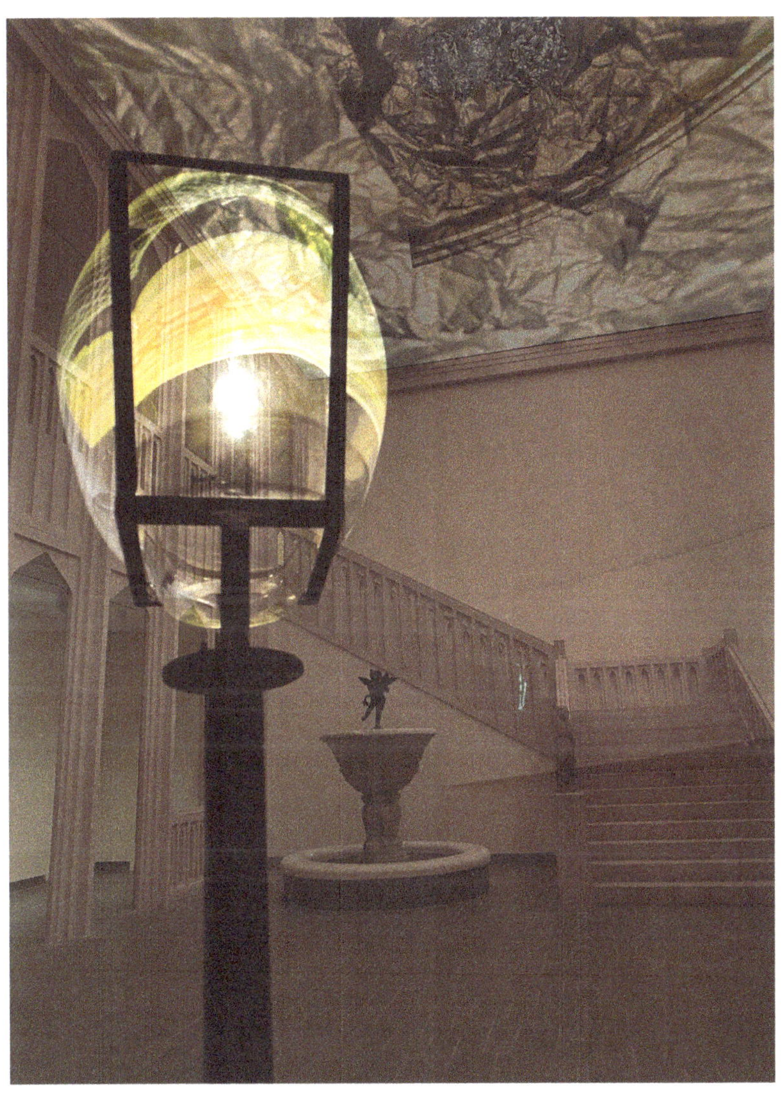

Open

J.W. Surface

After Chris Austin's "to be lost in the right direction" gouache painting on Arches paper

We first locked eyes
when you glided
through the doorway
of that abandoned building.

Your girth was beautiful.
I haven't been this in love
since I saw Constance's Streetlight,
or Kenton's perfect yards.

When I saw you,
I actually took a deep breath,
and quickly understood
how people could drop thousands
to hang you in their hallway,
above their bed,
in their library,
to keep you close,
to keep you to themselves.

Hunt or Curiosity?

J.W. Surface

After Chris Austin's paintings "I'll Hear You Calling Me" and "Courageous Wondering"

I.

The light cascades upon you,
baptizing you into divinity.

The woods
almost welcome you
more than the sea.
You belong here
just as much as you don't.

II.

What I would give to be hiking
among those trees,
in that baptizing light
and see you coming,
looking at me
like you look at those two unsuspecting doe
with that focus,
with those teeth,
ready to sink into flesh
and give a new sound of raw
to the forest.

Symbolic Self-Portrait

Breanna Emmett

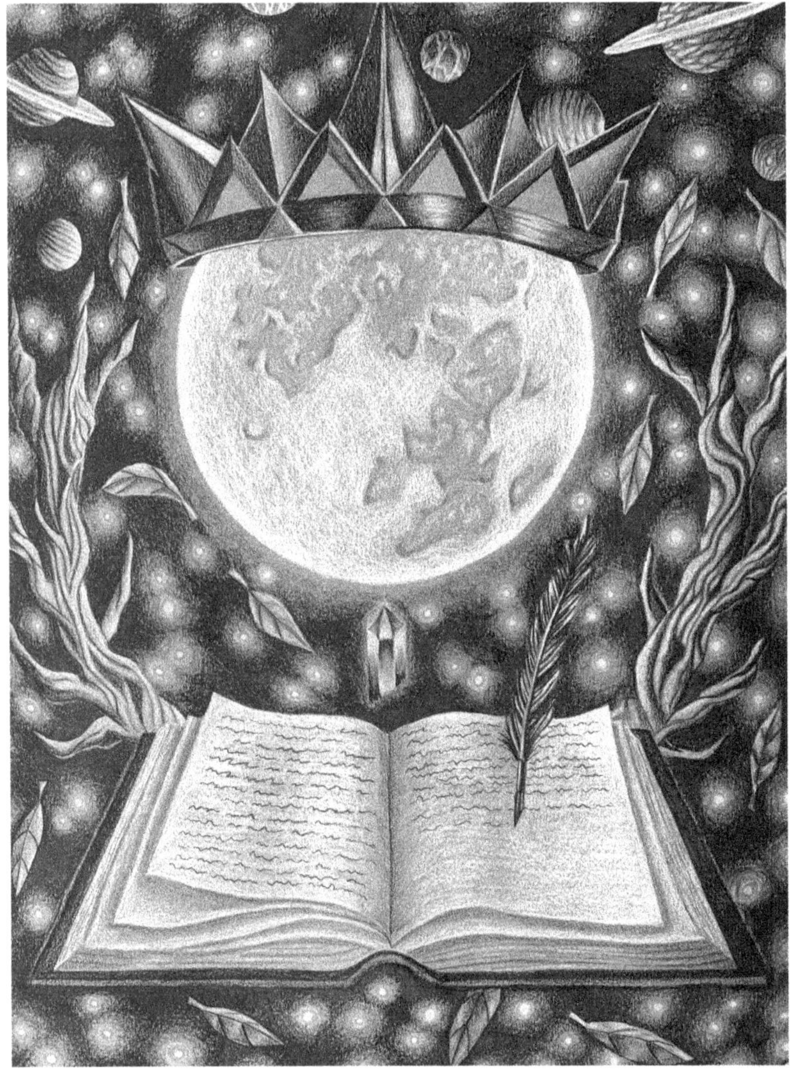

Grandfather's Amulet

Sierra Brooke Durbin

Emilia Nightingale always wondered why her grandfather's amulet possessed a mystical aura. As a little girl, she poked and prodded about the mysterious jewel that hung from the pocket of his wrinkled pair of slacks. Her grandfather was an odd man who mostly kept to himself, but he told her the most wonderful stories of evil wizards raising the dead and dragons setting little towns ablaze, probably things one shouldn't mention to an innocent eight-year-old. Her baby blue eyes sparkled in awe looking into the man's greying ones, which were hidden behind a pair of vintage copper frames. He was just as mysterious as that amulet. She wanted to know why he wouldn't part from it.

The majority of Emilia's childhood took place in that rickety, worn-down bookshop full of nifty little trinkets. Each summer she visited the quaint Victorian cottage house, she imagined she was a little witch in training, collecting rose petals, twigs, grass blades, and other pieces of the Earth for specifically concocted nature spells. While gathering ingredients, she would sneak glances inside her grandfather's study room whenever the door was ajar and notice him hunched over old journals or intently writing with his black feather ink pen. He was secretive and wise, like the wizards in his stories. She often wondered if he was conjuring up spells of his own.

The last time she spent a summer with her grandfather, she was just beginning her years at middle school. It felt like an eternity since she scrunched up her nose in protest to the accumulating dust in her grandfather's bookshop. Her parents did not like the influence he had on her growing up. It was their fear that she'd shelter herself away from society, spending every waking moment in a fantasy. With each approaching summer, Emilia begged her parents to drive her back to her grandfather's house. They refused her requests and encouraged her to make friends her age instead of hanging out with a loony, old man. Eventually, she stopped asking and obeyed her parents' wishes. She didn't realize it would all end so suddenly. Whenever she felt lonely and wanted to feel a connection with her grandfather, she imagined and reinvented the stories he told her as a child. She hoped, somehow, they could communicate through their dreams or at least make it known that she was thinking of him. Neither of them stopped believing that one day they would see each other once more.

Now she is eighteen and preparing to leave home again, but this time it's to a campus in another state. Inspired by his wild tales, she wished to travel and tell stories of her own. While her parents, and many other people thought he was crazy, she knew he was eccentric and innocently young at heart. Emilia wanted to spend one last summer with him before embarking on the journey of adulthood and leaving her child life behind. This time, she was able to drive herself down the winding roads far away from the city. The stars twinkled brightly as if guiding her way there. She wondered if the magic would be waiting for her.

He looked a little older, but everything else remained the same, even the ruby amulet dangling from his pocket. Emilia may have been taller, but she still felt small, losing herself in the vast collection of the shop. The wooden walls were adorned with strange but intricate tapestries with depictions of galaxies and symbols that seemed to represent life and death. Her eyes roamed over the shelves. One of them carried a row of uniquely shaped jars with cork tops covering the contents inside. Through the glass containers, she could see a variety of stones, some sort of herbs, and perhaps sticks of incense, which were used to make the shop smell like cinnamon in addition to the rich scent of aging books. An ancient, yellowed scroll stood in a glass case, wrapped in a red ribbon. A collage of framed exotic butterfly wings, vibrant and lifeless, hung in the corner above a large, rusted chest, which sat locked up without a key in sight. Each item had a story behind it. Her grandfather reminded her some of the stories she knew as a little girl. He explained that the scroll, if spread out, would reveal an ancient language unknown to man, and the pirate's chest was dug up from a faraway island, yet the key remained missing. To obtain obscure items such as these over the years was no easy task for one person alone. She intently listened as he confessed engaging in wild adventures with a diverse group of spellcasters, where each member wielded wands with stones possessing great powers that enhanced their magical abilities. He explained they were a strong, secret community that conversed through cryptic messages only fellow magic users and their allies could decipher. The wizards wore a symbol of a dying star, its explosion of fragments containing the different elements of the Earth. These details always stuck with her because she wondered if there was any truth hidden within these stories. The one treasure he never described acquiring, though, was his enchanting amulet.

"How come you've always carried that amulet with you all these years?" She brought it up one evening while they were sitting on the red velvet chaise lounge, sharing stories and drinking tea by the crackling fireplace. The warm colors from the flames danced on his face.

"Well," he turned to look at Emilia with a smile in his eyes, "it reminds me to hold onto the magic." He winked at his curious granddaughter. She couldn't help but smile back. He quickly changed the subject and the two conversed into the wee hours of the morning.

The sound of cicadas filled the crisp, cool nights. Leaves swayed with the breeze and drifted to the ground. The autumn colors seemed to glow when the sun set earlier each day, a sign that the stories were about to come to an end. Emilia promised she'd return the following summer to share some of her adventures with him. Each night, she was transported back to her grandfather's place in vivid dreams. She imagined she was outside the door to his study room, hearing the frantic flipping of pages on the other side. In the following scene, she passed through the barrier like a ghost. For the first time in her life, she could see inside the entire study room. There were candles lit beside the old man. He didn't notice her in the room with him and kept mumbling words under his breath like he was reciting some sort of chant. Before she could make her presence known, her eyes opened and her body was back in bed.

By winter, her grandfather went to dream much the same. Although, his body, arrested by time, found permanent slumber. He never woke up. The news of his passing plagued her with sadness. His life ending was like the death of her youth, yet her dreams continued. She could hear the crickets that hopped and sang in the side garden where she used to pick flower petals and red nightshade berries for her little elixirs. Her grandfather would pretend to sip them from a tea cup and toss the undrinkable liquid as soon as she turned her back. Those elixirs, she believed, were supposed to keep him alive forever. Her alarm brought her back to reality, a reality she wished she could escape. She longed to dream permanently so she wouldn't have to bear a world without her grandfather, the only person who ever truly knew her. As soon as the semester ended, she traveled back home to grieve with her family and make one last trip to his shop.

Entering the dwelling felt like she was stepping back in time. Upon hearing the little bell at the top of the door *ting*, her grandfather would scurry in to greet her, grinning from ear to ear underneath his bushy, white mustache. His eyes would light up like fireworks after seeing her return the same joy in her face. Picturing the past triggered tears to trickle down her cheeks. She sniffled, wiped her sleeve across her face, and pressed onward.

She wandered up the spiral staircase, steadying herself with her hand gliding along the curve of the iron railing. At night, the candle sticks on the staircase would light the path. The flickering lights would appear like they were floating in the darkness. Each step up was like walking on air. When she was little, she believed there were fairies twirling around the candles because shadows would move and morph in the gentle breeze of a passerby. Hovering above the little shop seemed like she was entering a different world. Two haunting shadows cast on the wall as she approached the last step. In front of her were two stone gargoyles perched on giant pedestals, guarding the upper level. Their protruding fangs could shred flesh and bite through bones.

Walking past rows of torn and tattered books, she made her way down the hall to her grandfather's special study. The sight of the arched cherry oak door reminded her how much he secured the room behind it like it held medieval chalices and mountains of gold coins. Tempted by her curiosity, like a little girl weary of breaking the rules, she carefully pushed the door aside. It creaked as it swung open to reveal a room covered with eccentric plants from the ceiling to the wooden floor. She couldn't believe her eyes. Every detail in the room matched the ones she imagined in her dreams. The vines intertwined around the bookshelves, which were elaborately decorated with whimsical carvings along the sides. Several books were stacked in front of the shelves like small towers, forming what resembled a castle. Crystals of varying colors and shapes hung from the stained-glass window like they were wind chimes. A long ebony oak staff with an oblong cavity rested against the antique chair, which was placed in front of the desk where her grandfather often meticulously rummaged through books. Out of the corner of her eye, the amulet grabbed her attention. It seemed to wait for her on the desk, shimmering in the sunlight. She felt drawn to it, enchanted by its presence. Emilia picked it up and ran her finger along the textured golden prongs holding the ruby in place. A phantom-like face suddenly started to take shape behind the stone. She stared in horror as it stared back at her, both frozen and unable to move. Her limbs numbed and the amulet began to slip out of her hand. Stuck like a statue, she helplessly watched the scene play out in slow motion. Her grandfather's amulet fell flat on the floor. *SMACK!* A burst of light pierced through the crack.

Emilia Nightingale was enchanted by an explosion of wild colors that suddenly burst through the amulet's cracked ruby like a lightning bolt striking up towards the heavens. The swirling cyan blue and amethyst purple blended with a fuchsia pink, throbbing like a child's kaleidoscope. Her grandfather's study transformed into a sunset sky with fluttering clouds that moved like waves of watercolor. She felt the breeze of the vibrant paint strokes whirling around her body with an intoxicating energy numbing her senses. She felt completely immersed in a breathtaking display of light resembling the aurora borealis. The colors flickered with sparks as they morphed in and out of each other. Sprinkles of glitter tickled her skin. This captivating scene felt like a dream, like her childhood imagination had finally come to life.

Within seconds, the show ended as the colors faded from existence. The world returned to normal, but a mystical presence lingered in the air. Nothing looked out of place, yet something within her seemed changed. The books on the wooden shelves were still caked in a thick dust and the amulet on the floor shined brightly as ever as sunbeams penetrated through the window. The reflection activated a dazzling iridescence, making the whole room sparkle. Her eyes followed the ray of sun, discovering that the amulet's injury had healed over. It was as if nothing had happened; then a letter drifted down from the ceiling with the stamped symbol of a dying star.

Little Black Box of Self

Breanna Emmett

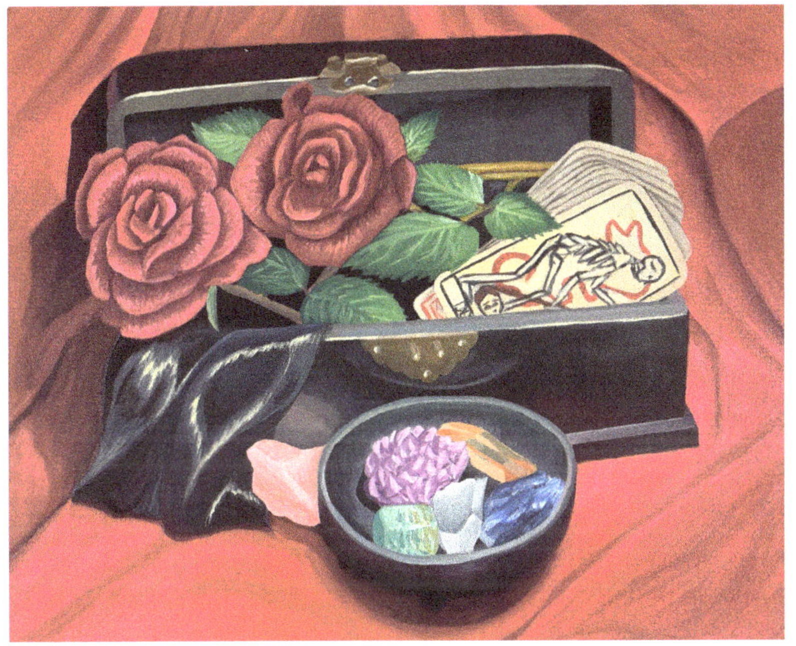

Styx, *River of Hatred*

Breanna Emmett

I think of you, and my veins turn
        into the river Styx.

Blood boiling, steam billowing thick
        enough to choke
        any lost soul who dares to travel
along its path. I think of you,

and feel
every broken
        promise
creeping up   my   spine,
        clutching

with long spindled fingers that pierce
        each vertebrae,
paralyzing me in a moment

fleeting and doomed
to forever collapse in on itself.

I think of you,
and between the realms of Gaia and Hades,
my spirit is pulled in both directions,

stretching itself thinner
and thinner with each beat
of the flowing river.

I think of you,
and uncertainty plagues my mind.

        I do not know which of us
                I would rather pull

                        to the bottom

                                of the Styx.

Where Is Water, Is Survival

Sarinitty Woodruff

There are rhapsodies swimming in the water
Milky streams casting out the light and shadows
of our histories, and my history makes me
decide how much I can carry on a thinly
threaded sling, as carefully as threading
a small-holed needle, who waits to prick
I don't need all of its anatomy fossilized
Some memories, some happenings
tore the anger of displacement into me,
in my own home, so they don't need memorials
They need to rot, unwoven, unlike life
along an itchy creekside, and instead, made
departed through octagonal patches of dirt,
which can't be sifted and the departed found bare
Found where? Let's find our buried languages
Those which are oral, musical, and patter like birds
in unmarked tombs, entangled within the moss
The vowels still echo like alluring sirens, but
no one pays the sounds attention, and
they drift until they drown, splashing
the next in line who's ready to disappear

Vertigo

Alyssa Todd

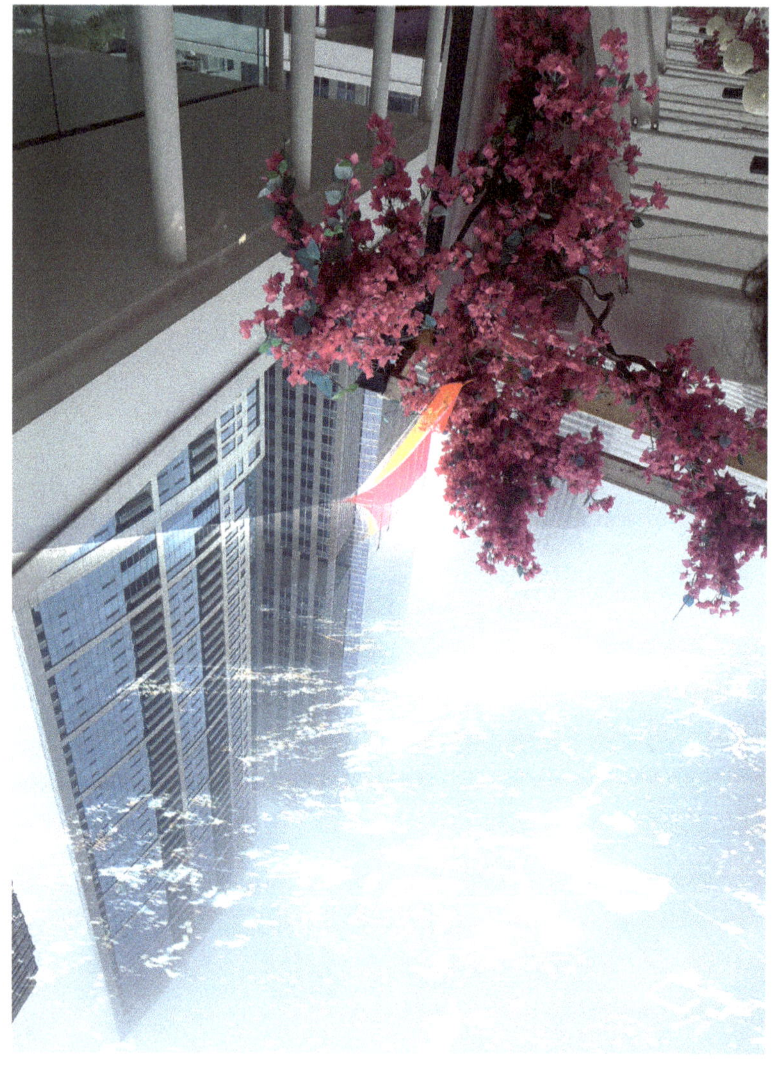

Not Until Then (A Climate Change Anthem)

Kenneth Shields

Please scan the QR code to hear the audio.

Beautiful Butterfly

Sydney Smith

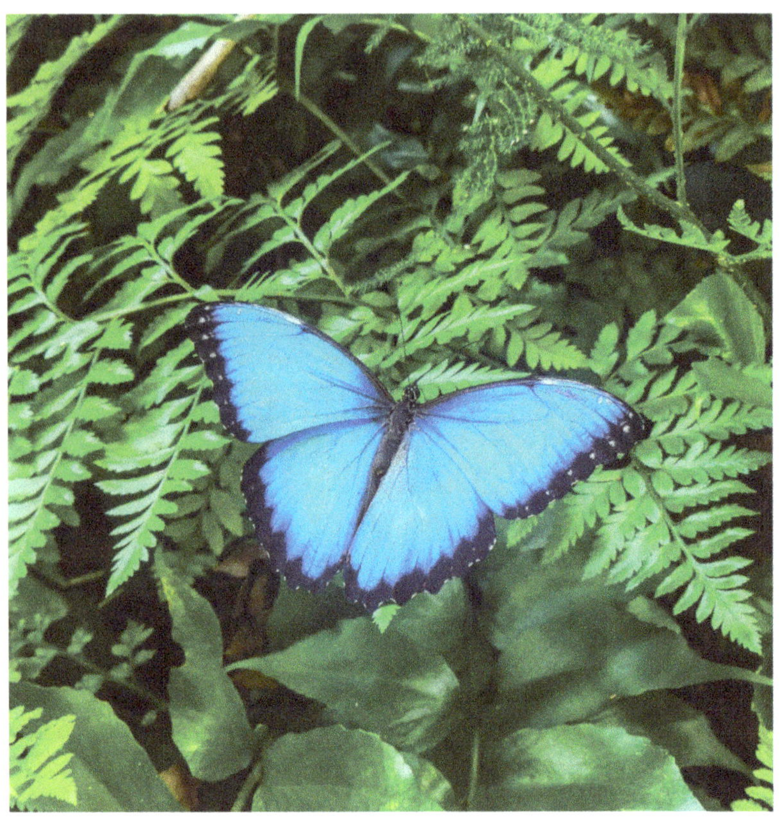

Lessons of a Spring Night

Christopher Schmidt

In their white robes, there is reveling under a royal sky
filled with piercing stars, declared to shine like the banner
they shroud themselves in—"see the 50 identical
points of white!" conservatively aligned like salt-boxes
in the suburbs.

I wonder; do the hoods have cosmic filters?
Do they obscure the billions of random rays
used by sea turtles and night flyers
to find their ways?
Is there no perception of the giants and dwarfs,
rainbows of brilliance, shifting red and sometimes blue
in their races to infinity?
Bright and dim, unimaginably gargantuan to unimaginably
        dense.
Some are swirls birthing suns
while others nova into nebulae, erupting out of
their senility and into tomorrow's primordium.

Is there reason to believe the light cast on fellow planets
Is used to see
only what is visible through slits in a sheet?
Are their night's skies dotted with fiery crosses,
proudly erected in declaration of fabled values?

Beyond the chanting and under a late Spring Polaris,
I watch a newborn loggerhead step into the lapping surf.
        Wide-eyed,
it accepts the chilly embrace from the tiniest plankton and
        the sequoia kelp,
and bravely swims with the others,
leaving the shore
and the flames
behind.

Ever Growing Love

Cambel Castle

you were like an overgrown wildflower field,
your garden of beauty and your leaves of love spilling out.
I would tend to you,
to our devotion.

pulling out the weeds,
gently replacing the soil.

tenderly I helped you to grow,
through the spring,
into the summer.

but then it started to get cold
frantically I picked your petals
desperately trying to save any part of you

instead,
there I stood with my feet in the snow,
looking at the remains of you in my arms,
drawing you close to my chest.

just as soon as I was able to feel you again
you crumbled into pieces in my hands
slipping through my fingers,
whisked away by the wind.

Beautiful Flowers

Alexis Darland

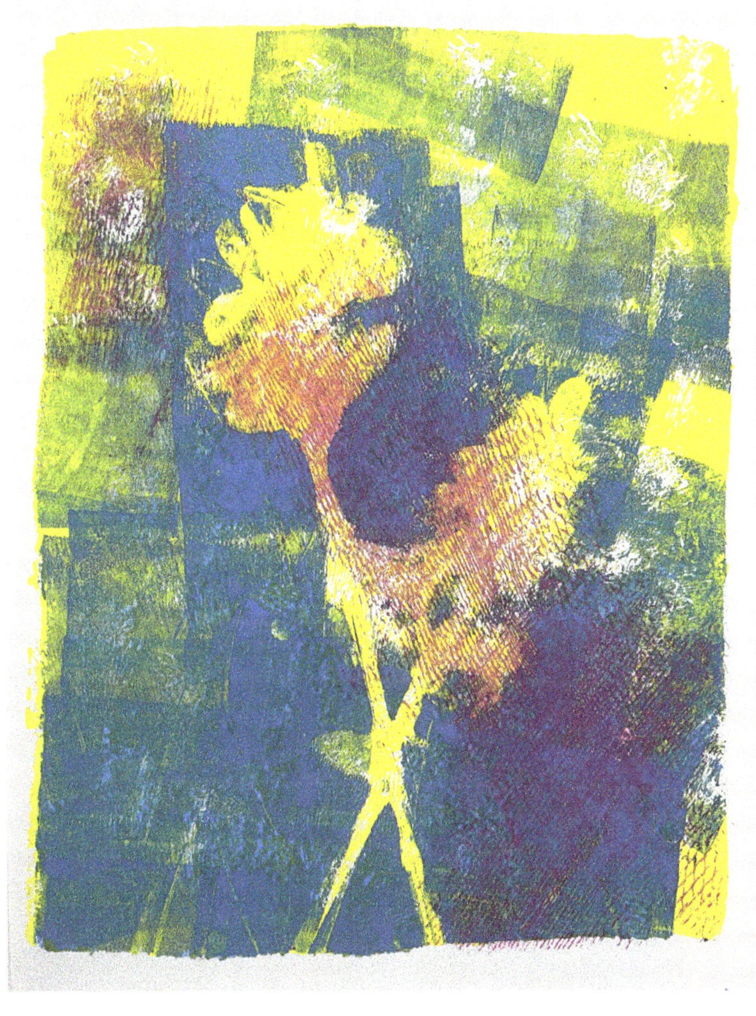

Strangers Bearing Flowers

A.V. Bailey

No amount of sorries
Made sense anymore
Gifts left unopened, letters I burned
If I never see you again,
It wouldn't be long enough

Geraniums and Orchids

Strangers to friends
Friends to lovers
And, in the blink of an eye,
Lovers to strangers
Funny how time can move backward
While still moving forwards

Oriental poppies and Dahlias

Our favorite songs whisper in my ears
Our favorite poems trace my fingers
Tears never have fallen so quickly
As the ones that could never forgive
Let alone forget

Baby's breath, Yarrows, Echinaceas

As you never stop begging
Saying it's not your fault
Oh, but it is
There never was much sense to
Strangers bearing flowers
So this is

goodbye.

Still

Cambel Castle

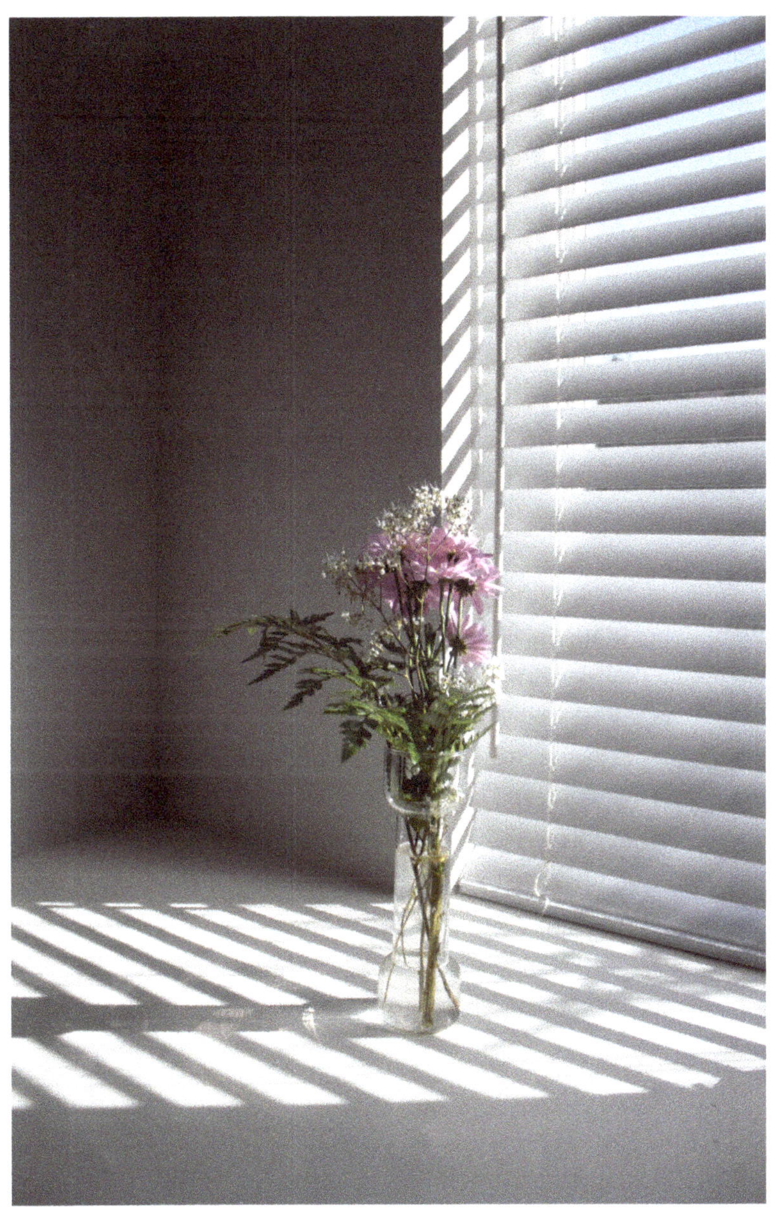

Why I Can't Hate You

Sabrina Camargo

You know you had something true when you can't hate it as
it abruptly leaves you
I can't hate you because you showed me what I deserve
And what I don't
I don't hate that I run into you and see your *gorgeous* smile
I hate that your smile became shy and sad when you
see me
I don't hate the cute little eye flutter when you see me
I hate that I miss the way your eyes looked into mine
as we laid in silence
I don't hate the cordial side hug
I hate that I miss your warm embrace that told me
you wouldn't let go
I don't hate that the place I call home is tainted with your
presence
I hate that I miss standing on the curb as you caressed my
cheek and pulled me in for a soft
goodbye kiss after it rained
I don't hate you because you ended things
I hate that they couldn't continue
But what I hate most, I hate that I can't hate you

until the spaghetti sticks

Riley E. Childers

to test if spaghetti is cooked
throw it at the wall
if it sticks
it's ready
if it falls
fill your time as it boils

we find ourselves entangled
like fettuccine twisted artistically on the plate
presented beautifully by a chef's hand
lost in the boils of time
dancing to the twang of country music
lingering in the kitchen
hoping that this moment never ends

this was our normal
filling our time as it boils
simple meals with prolonged laughs
casual panic ensuing when the smoke around us climbs the
walls
setting off the smoke alarm

we let go of each other
pasta water boils over
raining down the sides of the pot
steam rises
helping us fog up the windows

...

you open the window and toss me the towel
and I wave it like a white flag
signaling we are no longer stuck in each other's gaze

once all is said and done
we let out nervous laughs
then join each other again
I wonder if your thoughts pause
if there is an intoxicating feeling
that comes over you like there is for me

I don't need to ask
I just want to stay intertwined with you
like the noodles in the pot are with each other
I won't stop until the spaghetti *sticks*

Offering Heart

Cambel Castle

I was cold in the darkness and so were you.
so I built a fire to bring some warmth.
I would tend to the flames as you watched,

but soon watching wasn't enough.

you demanded it to be "bigger"
so I would add wood to the fire, log after log
to keep the embers from dying out,

but still it wasn't enough.

I cut my hair short, throwing the rest in the flames

"bigger"

I pulled at my clothes,
slowly I stepped out of my shorts and unbuttoned my shirt.
tossing them into the fire

"more"

I looked around, desperately trying to find anything else to
feed the fire,

but all that was left was you and me

so forward I stepped,
into the fire.

hot embers scolding my feet,
my skin bubbling and crackling,
flesh peeling from my bones.

...

flames devoured my body,
engulfing me,
swallowing me whole.

I burned myself to keep you warm.
but even with my body ablaze,
I'm still not a light in your life.

I looked up at you from the ground,
a pile of ash and soot,
your expression stone cold,

but your face changed when you saw a distant spark.
without a second thought,
you trampled trough me,
leaving a footprint in place of my heart.

My Body

Elizabeth Dubak

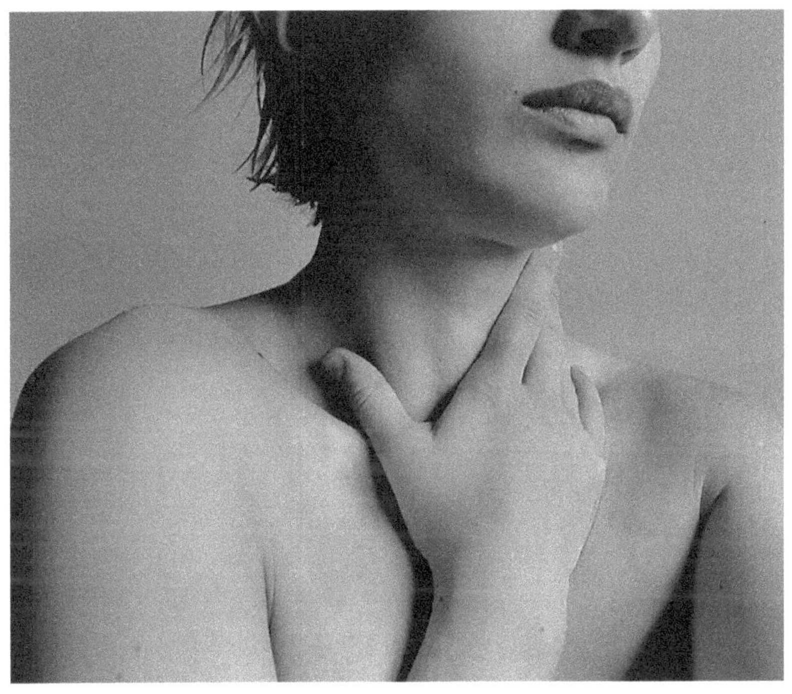

What Happened to the 90s?

Chase Rorie

even though i asked
i'll ask again
because maybe this time, i'll be heard
not just becoming another voice in the background
fading away, as others talk over me

what happened to wanting to get to know me for me?
watching my creativity flow like a river
empowering others to be the best version of themselves
being unapologetically them,
like i'm unapologetically me

what happened to asking questions i can answer?
because you are infatuated with how my brain works
giving you unhinged but clear answers
creating more of a mystery in the air for you to solve

what happened to wanting to hear me ramble?
about the things i'm ever so passionate about
painting a clear image in your head
so that you may see the world from my point of view

what happened to asking me deep questions about love?
& why i crave a soul to match mine
or why i want to be so spiritually intertwined
with the soul my heart finds so divine

i forgot
this generation is different
the deep questions aren't mentioned
because they're erased from the vision
"what's your body count"
that's all that seems to matter
to someone who won't care for you now
or not even in the realm we enter after

but i forgot
this generation is different
what only matters, is what's between your thighs
not where your heart & head is
so i guess
the conversations actually will be skipped
because all you care about?
is if i'm going to be the next body on your list

Wife Women

Emma Knaack

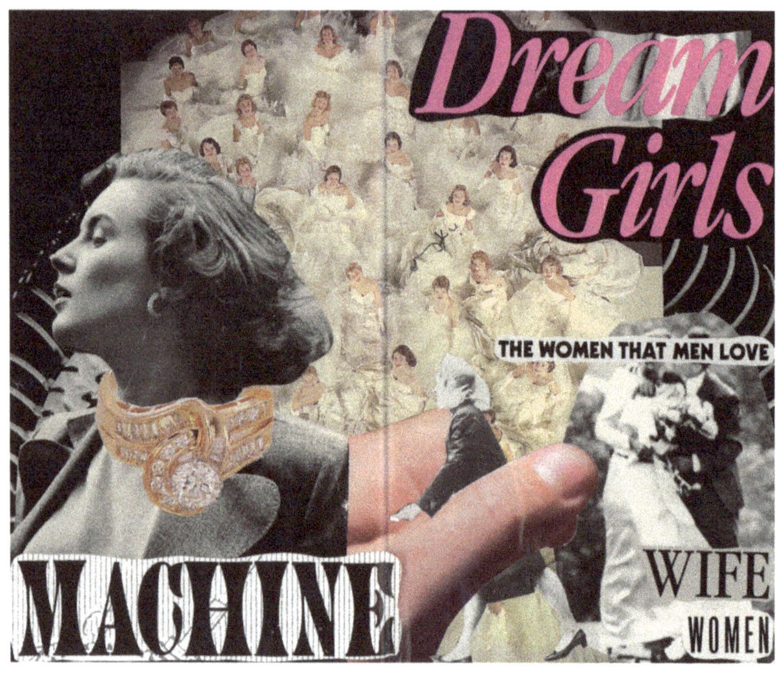

House of Cards

Maddilynn Meulen

This house we built
is bound to fall.

The foundation is weak
and the burden of being a house
is heavy.

It wasn't supposed to be like this.

Don't you feel the anxiety
when you walk up the steps?

Don't the hairs on your neck
stand at attention when you
hear a door open?

It wasn't supposed to be like this.

I loved it so much…
until the drywall started to crack.

Until the floors started to splinter.
until the foundation began to falter

We wanted to build something so badly
that we didn't care what we built it with.

So instead of trust,
we used lies, lust,
and a deck of playing cards.

So, please, stay with me
play a round of poker,
and watch as the roof
falls
in

Memento Mori

Alexis Darland

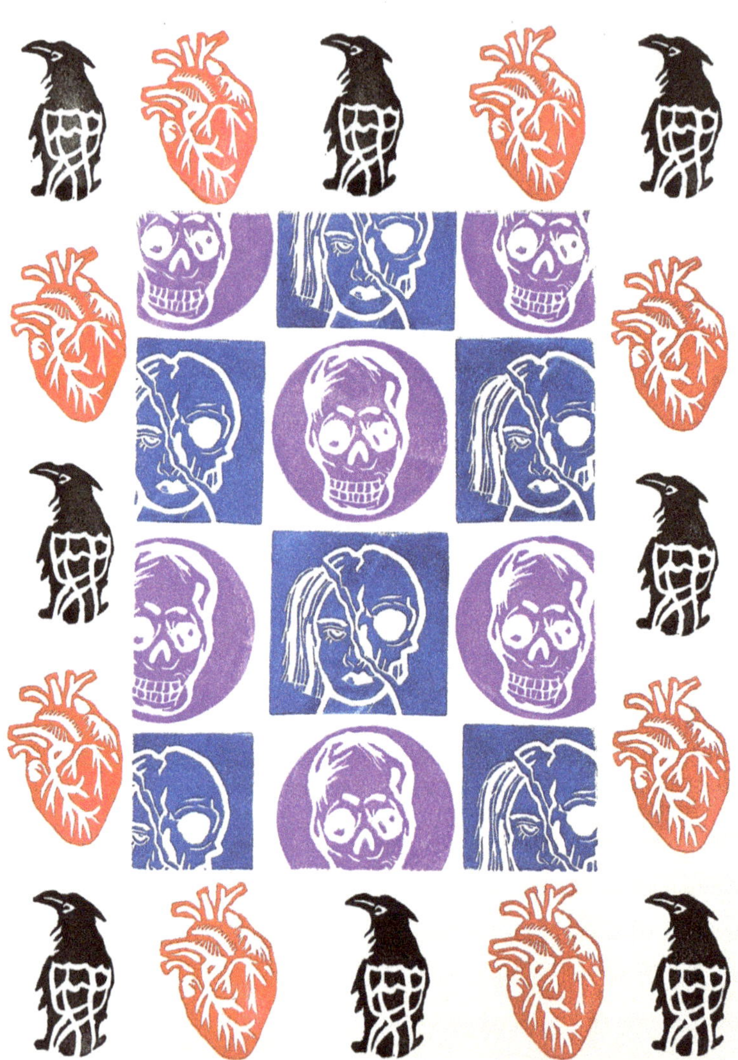

Writing Love Stories

Kaylan Gwyn

I don't think I know how to fall in love. I know what love is. I think I know what it means to be in love, but I just don't know how to get to there from here. Sometimes I can feel it. That deep aching in my chest when I see couples together or when I see a group of friends laughing. I can't quite tell if it's longing or heartache or loneliness, but I know that it comes from the part of me that knows that I've never had love like that. The part of me that is scared that I never will.

I think a subconscious part of me does know how to fall in love. I can feel it a little bit of it every time the cashier tells me I look nice today, or in the moments when I read love stories so vivid and beautiful that I can almost feel a hand caressing my cheek before the chill of the air reminds me I'm still alone. If I close my eyes and cup my face, it almost feels like someone else for just a moment and the world doesn't seem quite so painstakingly lonely.

I think there's another part of me that doesn't want to fall in love. The part of me that seeks out to read and remember the most heartbreaking, soul-sucking, emotionally scarring stories that I can find. I can remember the first angst story I read that really hurt the way I wanted it to. The main character overheard the other describing the man of her dreams and he just knew it was him, everything fit the description. He finally just knew that the love of his life loved him too, and so he confronted her. "I know you love me. I heard you say it and I just…I'm so happy. I love you too." It wasn't even tagged as angst, so I didn't even know it was going to hurt.

"I wasn't talking about you."

I could feel my own heart drop as the character's did. The realization of who the other character was actually talking about. The pain of being that vulnerable, to give someone the rope holding you afloat and them just dropping it. And you can't be angry at them. It's your own fault for thinking they were talking about you. Your own fault for thinking someone like them could ever love you. Could ever love someone like you, could ever love someone like me.

It's quite funny though, being this loveless second thought of a person. I can't tell you how many people I've given advice on their love lives. I've been told I give great advice, at least to other people. I'm not so great at advising myself, bit of a hypocrite I'd say. It's terrifying though how easily though that someone who's never had love can imagine heartbreak so definitely and imagine how to get out of it just as quick.

Well, that's a lie. I've had love. At least a type of it. Several types of it in fact. Usually the bad kinds though. The kinds where you have to lay on a couch, picking at my bleeding fingernails until they ache, as they ask again, "And you were how old when this all started?" I'm not sure what the answer is so I never answer, but I know it was long enough ago that I don't know or don't care to know if I can ever love again because of it.

But on the rarest of occasions, I've felt this shimmer of something different. Something so wonderfully, heart-wrenchingly horrible that I just adore it. That little glimmer of hope that makes that gnawing emptiness in my chest ache just a little less before it comes back painfully two-fold during the come down, and it hurts in just the right way that I can almost feel like I'm still a person, and not the shell I usually am.

It's crumpled, hidden somewhere deep in my chest behind scars and emptiness and burning, repressed emotions. Right there is the most beautiful little glimmer that actually feels like love until I remember to suppress it again. It's rare to come out. It usually hides itself in the videotaped laughs of friends I've not spoken to in years, in the smiles of people that could be friends if I wasn't so scared to think myself worthy of friendship. Those ones are easy to spot though. Easy to hide away as soon as I get scared by the fact I can't feel the emptiness eating me away from the inside.

You know where it's harder to spot. In stories like this. In stories I write just like this—

> I loved you with every shattered piece of my broken heart. I loved you like Achilles loved Patroclus. Like how Mr. Darcy loved Elizabeth and how Orpheus loved Eurydice. I loved you like all the famous lovers loved throughout all of history. I loved you like all the characters in your wonderfully sappy romance novels loved all their best beloveds. I loved you so much that we deserved to be memorialized throughout all of history for our love like all the famous lovers you pretended us to be.
>
> I wanted to spend the rest of my days by your side. I wanted to marry you every day and propose to you every night. I wanted to spend the rest of my days by your side and tell you everyday everything I adore the most about you, my best beloved.
>
> You finally taught me how to fall in love. I could feel it a little bit of it every time you told me I looked beautiful that day, or in the moments when you read me love stories so vividly and in that sweet, loving tone that I could almost feel caressing my cheek before the chill of the air brushed back against me. Then you'd lean down and kiss my head and for just the briefest of moments, the world didn't feel all that painstakingly cold anymore. I think there was a part of me that didn't want to fall in love before I met you, because it knew that nothing could ever compare to the feeling of your heart against mine.

Now, does that read like someone who's never felt the emotion they set out to describe? I certainly hope not. That'd ruin the whole story. But it's stories like that, that make that little glimmer, as much as I adore it, scare me that much more. Because how could someone so broken and alone write such beautifully heart aching stories and mean it. It just seems insincere, doesn't it? And that's what scares me. What if it's not?

That deep down there is a part of me that is so ready and so excited to feel all the emotions I fear the most and I've spent years keeping it at a distance. Think of all the people, all the friends, all the lovers I could've cared about and if there really is a part of me that can love like that, then I'm the one who's sabotaged every chance of happiness I could've ever had, sabotaged all the years I could've spent loving myself like that.

And if there isn't—then why do I set out to torture myself with the thought of an emotion I'll never get to experience in the way that feels right. They say it's better to love and have lost than to never love at all, but, after ripping every thread of love I've ever found out of my chest with the fury of a madman fearing for his life, I'm not sure if that's true. I don't know what's harder—falling in love, knowing that I'll just tear myself apart to get away from it or spending the rest of my life as a loveless person writing love stories.

R—

Sarinitty Woodruff

Last night I mistook the silence of the room for solace,
before I felt the heat of my face paint it, like
the rhododendrons cultivated by you, climbing
up to pinch my nerves, all invaded, because of the
silence, and because of your now clear portrait
in my foggy eyes, brought on by cycling guests
Guests' eyes moving neither up nor down nor forward
A furtive language meaning, "I'm hiding something"
I'm hiding something: a gut feeling, and how I see
your beauty in their quick smiles when they speak of you
In the arrangement and formerly residing joy of the
estate, and within the missing parts of your story—
His story, but I maintain it's a matter of cold feet
They're young doubts with light weights
But, when I walk far past the wood to the shoreline,
I can see myself underwater too, like you, for too long
Sooner or later, I say, **R***ebecca*, I say, *this is all wrong*

Debussy and the Dream of Civilization

Alec Cizak

Endorphins
did not exist

until Debussy
taught a piano

to cradle panic
into a stupor.

Cat Lover

Lylanne Musselman

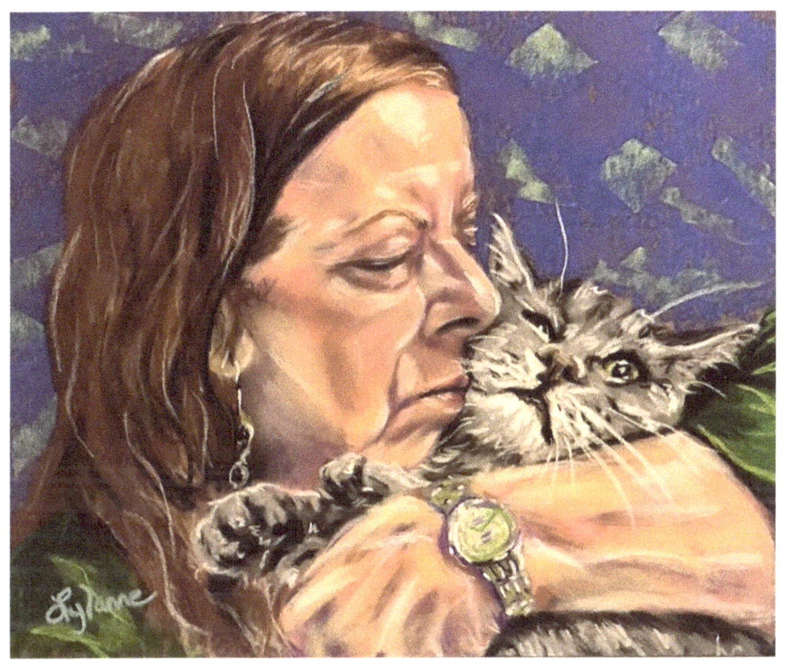

flapjacks are pancakes

Riley E. Childers

a journey to you
would require a trip across the sea
for some reason
that people don't understand
I'm willing to go miles away from here
to get to you

our constant teasing has no ends
fighting over the meanings of words
like your crunchy flapjacks being oven baked
made up of oats, butter, and syrup
and mine being a stove top meal made from
flour, eggs, butter, milk, and sugar
topped with delicious maple

we planted these seeds years ago
and just like a garden filled with ripe vegetation
our roots continue to run deep
their sweet starts keeping us grounded
in the same dirt thousands of miles away
just like the plants
if we get cut down
our friendship builds us back up

never have I questioned us
the us that can't stand side-by-side
physically but magically
we have found a way
to tether our souls from what seems to be
two different worlds
If I travel the sea will you promise
to sit across from me?
If you keep to your word
I promise to buy you flapjacks that are *pancakes*

Ode to my Parents

Maddilynn Meulen

Every year that I age,
older and older,
the more I understand
the woman my mother
had to become
and the sacrifices it entailed.

Groceries and baby clothes
replaced visits to the mall.
Free time became
something of the past.

I never got to know her
as a carefree teenager.
I never got to see my
parents as fools in love.

I have a recurring dream…
        One where my mom and dad
        aren't my mom and dad.
        They were kids,
        not kids with a kid.

I see them before
the weight of a child
beat them down.
                        Before the world chewed them up
                        and spit
                                    them
                                                out.

I watch the boy drive in that
        Stankin' Lincoln
I've heard so much about.
I stand by as the boy pulls up
        with hearts for eyes
And the girl gets in his car
        with butterflies in her stomach.
…

I see them at their happiest.

A Glance

Cambel Castle

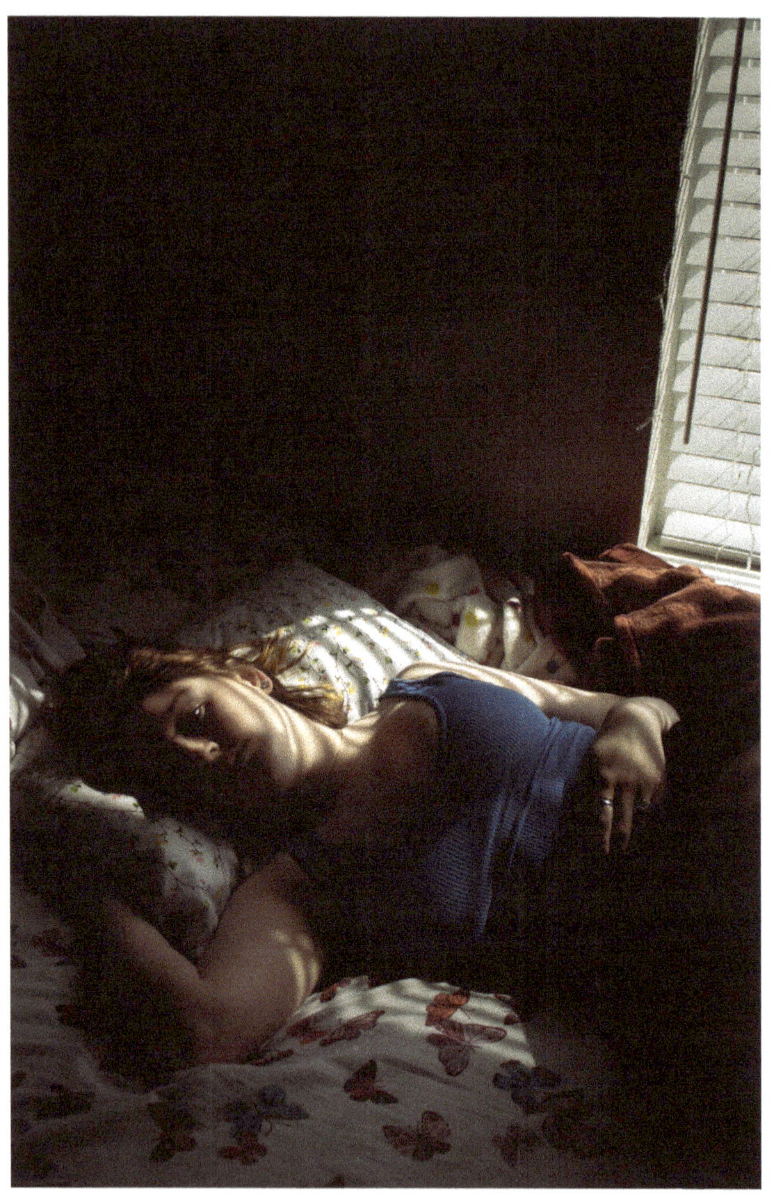

I Want a Home

C.S. Carrier

I want a fireplace. With a mantel.
Where I eat olives & read books against the flames. A wood-
stove would work.

I want chickens. Fresh eggs are electric.
I want sourdough baking in the oven. Beer ferment-
ing in the pantry.
I eat my bread, drink my beer after raking the leaves. That
way, I'm never empty.

I want mountains. The snow piling up on my birthday.
My birthday is in January. It's December now. It's always
December.
I want a lake house. Mist hovering above the glass.
Where water laps a canoe.
My lifejacket is orange.
I want a bathroom tiled over with blue tile. Because I
want to feel underwater
without being underwater.

I want intellectual futures, distributed cognition.
I want my body in a relationship with its environment.

I want poetry, the alchemy of its rooms. I want its
disruption. Which opens
my grammar, my blood, coded by toxic masculinity.

...

I want to be turned to a tree. To give air.
I want Dawn. I want Dawn because I love her.
She believes that I'm possible.

I want a record player because record player is cool.
To hear *A Love Supreme*
as it was, to listen to it as it is. There's something intimate
about a record player.

I want a bed. Where I can hide from migraines.
The sadness that comes from money.
I want to be valuable for the person I am, not the job
I do.

I want the windows full of azaleas, butterfly weed.
Full of monarch butterflies, all of the genders. Dreams that
haven't been named
yet. Those dreams that can't be named.
I want a place where I can cry. A place where I can
listen to others.

The Bridge

Julia Johnson

CW: Attempted Suicide
Dorlis Gott Armentrout Winner

It's snowing. Of course it is.

I pull my sedan over on the side of the road and slip out of the car. Shivering, I trudge through the wet slush up the bridge. *Squish. Squish. Squish.* Cars roar past me on the highway and I get a couple of strange looks. My eyes scan the giant stretch of metal and concrete, the only thing that stands between those cars and the watery death below. Finally I see it: a shiny new section of guardrail about a third of the way across the bridge.

The only sign anything ever happened here. A shiny new section of guardrail. I wonder when they replaced it.

It must have been sometime after February 3rd.

There shouldn't have been anything unusual about that February 3rd, except the fact that my older sister Opal came to my apartment for a surprise visit. I usually equate surprise visits with being told by the dentist that you have a cavity.

Surprise visits from Opal, on the other hand, I equate with being told by the doctor that you have cancer.

"So…how many days have you left these here?"

Opal nudged the sweaty laundry pile with her toe.

"If you don't like it, the laundry room is down the hall." I didn't turn away from my laptop.

"I'm trying to help you. If you leave those too long they'll smell like sweat forever."

I heard her moving around behind me. I ignored her and kept typing. She picked up the framed photo on the bookshelf. "You're still with Andy?"

"Yeah. So?"

"You don't have to snap at me; I was just asking."

"I didn't snap at you."

"You were definitely snapping at me!"

"I was just talking to you!"

"You don't need to yell!"

"Fine." I sighed. "Opal, I'm really busy right now. Andy and I have been going strong for thirteen months, so will you just let me do this?"

"If you really want to date him, I can't stop you…"

"Opal, what is your problem!" I finally turned away from my screen.

"What the heck are you doing on that?"

"Don't change the subject—"

"How can you even concentrate with that many tabs? How much homework do you even have?"

"Look, we can't all be perfect teacher's pets who turn in our assignments a week in advance—"

"Is that what you think of me? I'm just a teacher's pet? I work hard, unlike some people, and I don't procrastinate with eighteen Instagram tabs!"

"If you really want me to get stuff done, you'd get out of here and leave me alone!"

"Fine!" Opal grabbed her coat and keys and slammed the door. Her stomping footsteps echoed all the way down the stairs.

"Wait!" I almost said it. But I pressed my lips together and stopped the words from coming out. Right now, Opal would be like a shark. Admitting weakness would be like blood in the water. I could always call her later.

As soon as she left, it started to snow.

That snow covered a patch of ice. And Opal's car slid on that patch of ice, broke through the guardrail, and plunged into the river.

I found out two hours later.

I broke up with Andy the next day. He got a new girlfriend two days later, so maybe Opal was right about him. I broke up with my friends too. We haven't talked since Opal died. Why would any of them talk to me? I killed Opal. I should be in prison.

A few days ago, I decided I deserve worse than prison. I think I deserve the death penalty.

I won't get another shot at this. My old roommate Bethany has been following me around for the past couple weeks. She somehow found out that I sold my laptop. I couldn't touch that thing after I killed Opal. I told Bethany I bought a new one, but I don't think she believes me. She won't leave me alone now; she keeps following me to lunch and my apartment and my classes. I don't know how she makes it to her own classes. I told her I was going to get gas today and she wanted to come. I only shook her off by telling her I was actually going to wait until tomorrow. When she finally left, I ran to the car and practically squealed the tires to get out of there.

I won't get another shot. I lean on the shiny new guardrail and the cold metal stings my ungloved palms. I stand there until my hands go numb from the metal and the wind. I swing my legs over the top and stand on the outside edge of the bridge.

It's really slippery here. I might fall. My heart thumps. Why I am so nervous? Wouldn't that be easiest, just to fall by accident?

I wait for a few minutes, but my feet stay stubbornly stuck on the guardrail. Guess it'll have to be on purpose. Wind howls in my ears and snow crunches behind me. I won't get another shot. I open my hands.

A split second of terrifying, dizzying, leaning forward, about to fall…

Someone grabs my wrist.

I shriek and my feet actually do slip off. I shriek again, I'm falling for real but I don't want to go, I grab on to whoever it is and hope they don't let go…

I'm dangling there, suspended over the rushing river, holding on by one hand. My screams fill my ears.

"I've got you! I've got you!" Whoever it is is pulling me up up up, away from the water and up to the bridge, my feet find the guardrail and I scramble over it and cling the pavement. We're both panting, lying in the snow, feeling the cars vibrate the pavement as we catch our breath.

When my body stops shaking enough for me to move, I push my face out of the snow.

"Bethany!?"

Her teeth clack together. "I c-c-couldn't…couldn't l-l-let you…"

"I know."

Her teeth keep chattering.

"And…" I wrench the words from my abdomen. "I'm glad you didn't."

ode to the can of manwich that collected dust on the pantry shelf

Sarah Cunningham

my mother never made it
i yearned for the sauce that the cylindrical metal encased
there is just something about the word *manwich*
the way the portmanteau pops playfully
the way it feels full in my mouth

i longed for the can of manwich
some days i would stand in the pantry doorway
mesmerized, breathless, fixed
oh can of manwich, why must you collect
dust on the pantry shelf?

it wasn't until i realized the meat wasn't
already in the can, that
a house isn't a home if a family isn't living in it,
that the seasoned tomato sauce was in need of unification
 with
ground beef, cooked to eat, quick and easy for an esurient
 family

without proper nourishment you will remain unfulfilled
"a sandwich is a sandwich, but a manwich is a meal,"
smiles lining each side of the kitchen table
a side of cherry kool-aid and oven-baked fries
at least that is what i imagine if my mother made it

it is said, you become what you are around
i think i want to be that can of manwich
no, i know i want to be that can of manwich
then i realized, i am that can of manwich
idle, desired, but never pursued

Hopscotch

Danni Conn

Chalk was not on my list,
but when I passed by it in the store
all I could think about was my childhood.

It wasn't all that great,
but when we drew hopscotch on the pavement
I knew it was going to be a fun day.

Numbers all the way up to 10.
Bouncing from 1 foot to another.
Laughs filling the neighborhood.
Sweat rolling down our backs.

We would write swear words
thinking we were the coolest kids
on the block.
But then we would cross them out
so Mom would never know.

The day would be over,
but the memories stayed
written in every color.

The morning came
and everything was gone.
It had rained during the night.

I grabbed the chalk
and walked to the register.

The Old Beech Tree

Alec Cizak

That old tree
guarded our backyard,
a sentry standing
longer than the
civilized wilderness.

Cardinals nested among
the traffic of Rorschach limbs,
their brief lives a wonder
to that old tree.

Did arrogance
plague that old tree,
centuries rooted, solid,
convinced it would survive
the American comedy?

Lightning struck,
the 1995 tornado,
slicing that old tree
down the middle,
the weaker half
scooping out
a neighbor's roof.

The insurance man
deemed it a sacrifice
to the gods of premiums
when his boss ordered
that old tree's execution.

Naked land now marks the spot
where that old tree snubbed
the fleeting, the mortal.

What thoughts
occupied that old tree
as a chainsaw's teeth
chewed out its heart
and folded its trunk
to meet the earth
to be parceled
for the fireplace
it once smirked upon
from a mile above.

rough boy

Sarah Cunningham

i saw a black man cry today
silent, graceful, sublime
you don't see it everyday
but i saw it
a single tear rushed down
like a brook of honey
carrying fragments of the tears that never
saw the light of day

and why is that?
that black man and many more carry
the burden of an unrealistic expectation
to maintain minimal expression
to overcome cultural expectations
rooted in generational self-hatred

convinced with thinking that vulnerability equates
to depleted masculinity and being
a soft boy
nobody wants a soft boy
they want a big boy, a buff, rough, tough boy
one that holds everyone down even though no one is holding
him down

Reflections

Sydney Pinkstaff

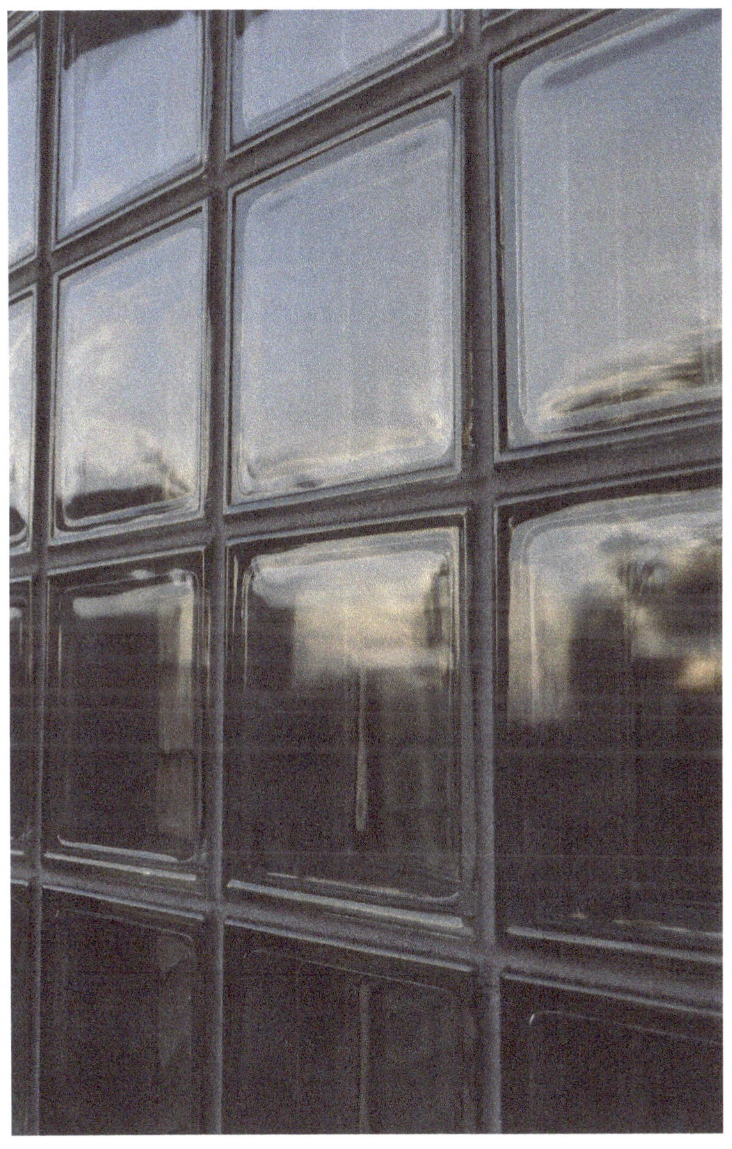

The Colors of the Rainbow

Sydney Pinkstaff

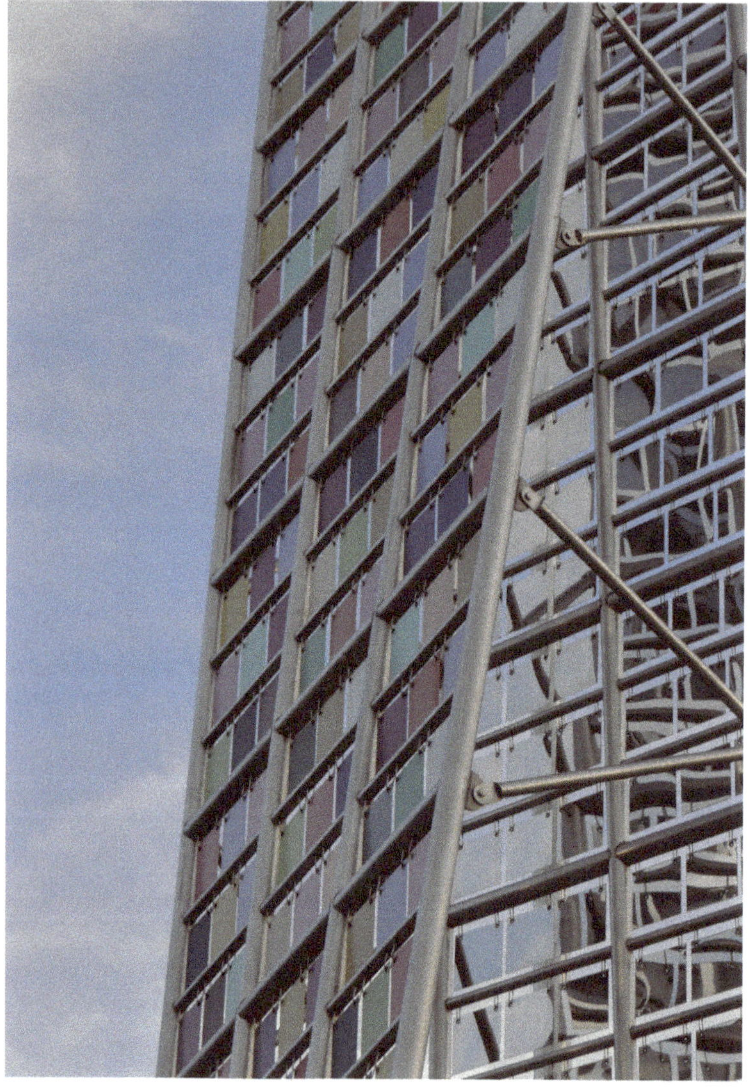

New Orleans

C.S. Carrier

I watched brass bands, blue trumpets
I bumped into bachelor parties, chiropractors, jugglers
I smelled vomit, old alcohol, smoke from grates
Spanish moss was swallowing the oaks

I passed a broken umbrella, pizza crust in a gutter
Mardi Gras beads entangled in power lines, balcony railings
I saw graffiti, flyers for missing cats
snakes in black spray paint

there was Joan of Arc in gold on a gold horse in traffic
an empty pedestal for Robert E. Lee, one for Jefferson Davis
there were magnolias in cemeteries, air in salt
jasmine in fences, I brushed their little amulets

I ate grilled oysters, pickled onions
I drank wine in a porcelain market with poets
I followed them to a theater darkened with smoke
where they read poems with weighted subjects

there was a sound that smoldered between us
it was a sound I'd forgotten, it was the sound of love
I tried to listen to it again, to let go my loneliness for a spell
& I've been trying to listen to it ever since

What Lies Ahead

Logan Wong

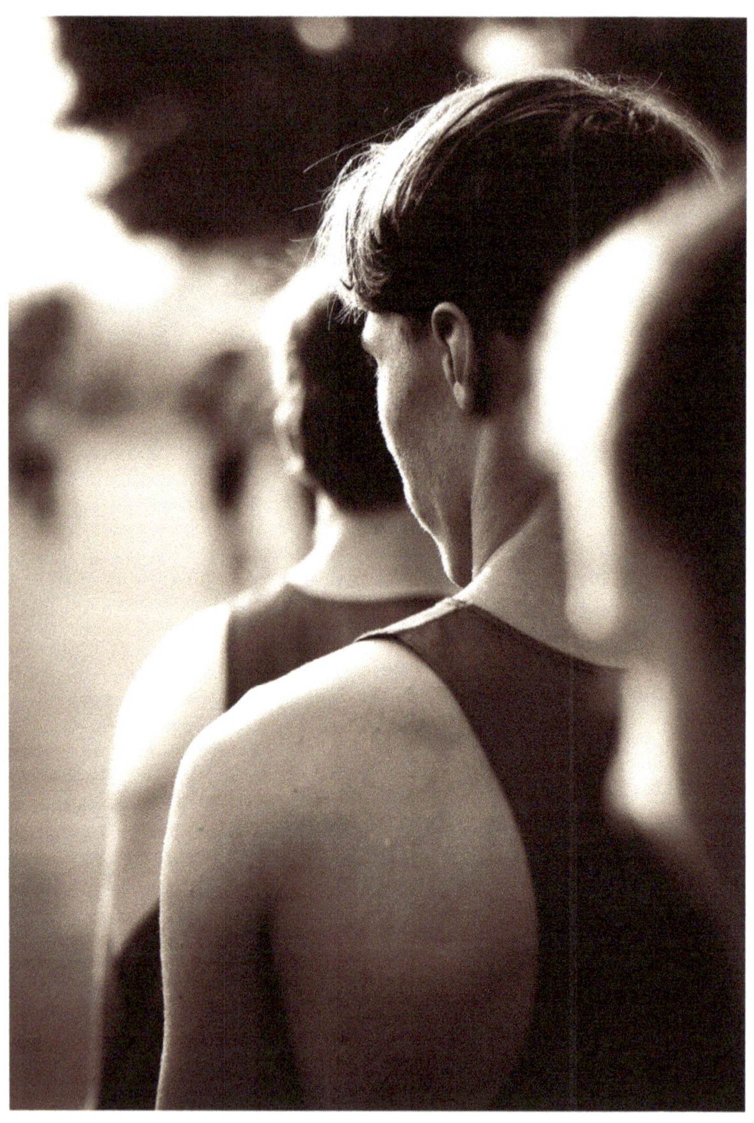

Where My Dogs At?

Logan Wong

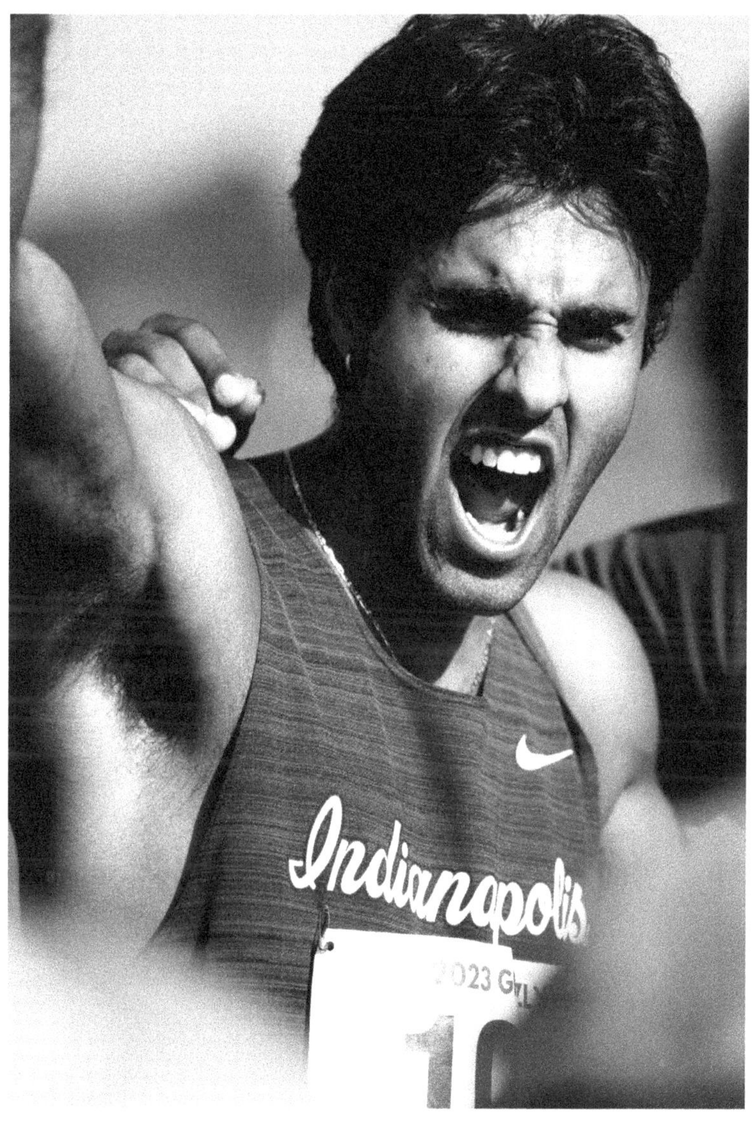

Campus

Sedna Deneb Bello Cordova

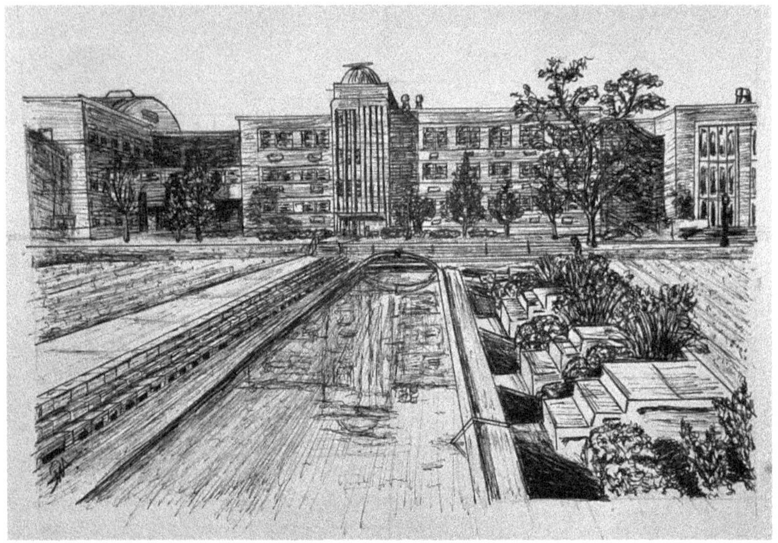

Contributor Biographies

Alec Cizak is a writer and filmmaker from Indiana. His latest collection of crime fiction short stories, *Nobody's Coming Home*, will be available from ABC Group Documentation in November of 2023.

Alexis Darland grew up in a military household, which led to her pursuing a career in art therapy because she saw how veterans hold in emotions. Her goal is to help veterans and prove everyone can be an artist.

Alrielle Viewegh is a recent UIndy graduate who is now teaching freshman English at Columbus North High School. She hopes to create an impact through writing and supporting her students.

Alyssa Todd is when the if because they yes also but so we you ok no therefore however happens maybe.

Amber Phillips is a sophomore professional writing major with a minor in legal studies. She is planning on following her fascination with fiction whilst stuck in the law libraries in the next few years.

A.V. Bailey is a junior double majoring in English and secondary education with concentrations in honors and mild interventions. When she is not studying, you will probably find her reading, writing, or dominating in Mario Kart.

Breanna Emmett is a senior majoring in art and creative writing. She spends her time pursuing her creative interests, all while making graphics and taking photos for *The Reflector*. She especially loves her cat, Edgar "Poe Poe."

Cambel Castle loves to create art, whether that be photography, art journaling or poetry. Expressing yourself through art is something you should try at least once.

Camille Dobbs is a junior studying English and minoring in psychology. She writes essays and poetry. She likes to shop, hangout with friends, and everything music! Her goal is to become an editor and currently works in the Writing Lab.

Christopher Schmidt is an anthropology faculty member who has published several peer-reviewed articles and written and/or co-edited four books on biological anthropology. He was an English major as an undergraduate student and has enjoyed fiction writing his entire life.

C.S. Carrier grew up in western North Carolina. He has degrees from the University of Massachusetts Amherst and the University of Louisiana at Lafayette. He was a drummer for the Arkansas band Thisness. He lives in Indianapolis, IN.

Danni Conn is an openly bisexual trans man who has had a rough journey but finds peace in words. He likes to write about love and heartbreak but has never been in an actual relationship.

E. Alexander Phillips-Hedge is a professional writing major with minors in creative writing and religion. He is the Managing Editor of *Etchings* and the Editor Manager of *Slapstik Comedy Magazine*. He enjoys thinking about the finer intricacies of life.

Elizabeth Dubak is a pre-art therapy major at UIndy. She enjoys photography and working out in her free time.

Emily Ratliff is a senior English and philosophy major minoring in history. She is a student ambassador in the Office of Advancement. In her free time, Emily is with friends, her pets, or advocating for reproductive justice and animal rights.

Emma Knaack is a senior professional writing and creative writing major minoring in business administration and concentrations in TELL and honors. She is the creative writing RSO president and a member of Phi Alpha Epsilon.

Hniang Te is an undergraduate studying exercise science pre-athletic training. She has a heart for capturing the beautiful moments and special days of lives through the lens.

Julia Johnson is a pre-physical therapy sophomore at UIndy. She loves Jesus, dogs, baking, and reading engrossing fiction. Julia thanks her mother for encouraging her creativity and encourages all of you to spend time doing something creative today.

J.W. Surface is an alumnus. He teaches high school mathematics and writes poetry and fiction when he isn't chasing his daughter around the house. He is indebted to God for blessing him and to his wife for putting up with him.

Kaelyn Stettler is an art therapy major. She has found a passion for ceramics. Kaelyn plans to attend UIndy for her master's program in art therapy to pursue a career that combines art making and healing.

Kaylan Gwyn is a transfer student. They've spent their life dedicated to education and creative writing. They are inspired by their mental health and the good in life. They are a believer in the butterfly effect, hoping to positively affect many lives.

Dr. Kenneth Shields is a Visiting Assistant Professor of Philosophy. His research focuses on the philosophy of autism and neurodiversity and it has been published in *Neuroethics* and the *Rowman & Littlefield Handbook of Bioethics*. He also has a bachelor's in music education.

Kensi Skaggs is an art and design illustration studio major, and this is their junior year here at UIndy. They have had an amazing experience learning art here and look forward to continuing to learn in the upcoming semesters.

Lilli Keiper is a junior at UIndy majoring in graphic design and minoring in marketing. She enjoys drawing, designing, photography, and making of any kind.

Logan Wong is a senior at UIndy majoring in communication with a concentration in electronic media and a minor in photography. He loves sports photography because he gets to capture some inspiring and exhilarating moments.

Lylanne Musselman is an alumnae, award-winning poet, visual artist, and playwright. Musselman has exhibited her art work at many exhibits. She has published poems and seven chapbooks. Lylanne is the president of the Muncie Artists Guild and is the director of Blackford County Arts Center.

Maddilynn Meulen is a junior majoring in English with a concentration in creative writing. She spends her free time writing, and then deleting, then writing again. She hopes to continue publishing her works and could really use a cup of coffee.

Chase Rorie has been writing poems for a year now and the poems submitted are poems from the poem book they are writing called *The Life Within a Poet's Eyes*.

Olivia Cameron is a senior creative writing and professional writing major. She hopes to get her MFA in fiction writing following her graduation from UIndy.

Raegan Brinson is a senior graphic design student at UIndy who loves every green.

Reid Bannec is a junior at UIndy studying visual communication design/graphic design.

Riley E. Childers is working on her Master's in English at UIndy. Her work has appeared in *Etchings Literary and Fine Arts Magazine*, *Doug Ramspeck's Under Black Leaves*, *Robin Lee Lovelace's Savonne*, *Not Vonny*, and *Tipton Poetry Journal.*

Sabrina Camargo is an alumnae. She has worked in the Office of Admissions as an Admissions Counselor on the Diversity Recruitment Team. She enjoys reading and writing poetry in her free time. She is also passionate about anything related to sociology!

Sarah Cunningham is a nursing major and she minors in creative writing and psychology at UIndy.

Sarinitty Woodruff is a UIndy sophomore who is always in the submissions process. She concentrates on writing poetry and poetic fiction. When she's not writing, she's looking at maps in expensive books, and flower catalogs, and improving the mediocrity of her music skills.

Sedna Deneb Bello Cordova is a first-year visual arts graduate student seeking to showcase her talent while growing professionally. She is an international student from Mexico. It is her goal to grow her career and create art.

Sierra Brooke Durbin, known online as "Sierrallstar," is a senior creative writing major and music minor. She loves expressing herself through content creation, songs, and fashion. Sierra performs in Crimson Express, is the VP of the Creative Writing and Film RSOs, and writes articles for *Her Campus*.

Sydney Pinkstaff is an art major and likes to do art things.

Sydney Smith is a junior at UIndy studying communication with emphasis in electronic media and public relations. In her free time, Sydney loves to take photos and show people that there is beauty in simplicity throughout her work.

Call for Submissions

Etchings Magazine 36.2, Spring 2024
Submissions due at 11:55 pm EST on
Wednesday, January 31, 2024

Guidelines for Submission:

- All UIndy students, faculty, staff, and alumni are invited to submit.
- All accepted undergraduate prose and poetry submissions will be considered for the Dorlis Gott Armentrout Award.
- Up to three short stories, creative nonfiction essays, or scenes, five poems, five visual materials, and five audio files may be submitted.
- **Visual**: for best print results, consider the 5.5 x 8 portrait page with .25 margins and flatten files to 300 ppi *.tiff CMYK 8 bit files.
- **Poetry, Prose, & Scenes**: present poems as single-spaced, prose double-spaced, and scenes following the genre's script conventions. All submissions formatted in Microsoft Word (.docx or .odt) in a 12-point font.
- **Audio**: submit *.mp3 files, and present scores/lyrics/spoken word following the guidelines for visual or poetry submissions above.

Etchings Magazine has a blind submission process, so please do not include any personal identifiers in your submission files (this information will be provided through Submittable).

Learn more about Etchings Press at etchings.uindy.edu
Submit work at etchings.submittable.com.

We do not accept email submissions. Please create a free account at submittable.com or sign in using Facebook.

For questions, email us at etchings@uindy.edu.
Follow us @uindyetchings on the platforms below:

www.ingramcontent.com/pod-product-compliance
Lightning Source LLC
Chambersburg PA
CBHW050011040726
47599CB00014B/1319

9781955521123